THE GOALS
THAT CHANGED
AUSTRALIA

THE GOALS THAT CHANGED AUSTRALIA

STORIES FROM
THE BIGGEST STAGE ON EARTH

David Weiner

FAIRPLAY
PUBLISHING

First published in 2024 by Fair Play Publishing

PO Box 4101, Balgowlah Heights, NSW 2093, Australia

www.fairplaypublishing.com.au

ISBN: 978-1- 923236-15-8

ISBN: 978-1-923236-16-5 (ePub)

Design and typesetting by Leslie Priestley

Front cover photographs:

Justin Setterfield, Getty (Cortnee Vine); John Aloisi (John Aloisi)

Other photographs:

Alen Delic, Mohamed Farag, Patrick Hoelscher, Aleksandar Jason, Matt Kay, André Krüger,

Bonita Mersiades, David Weiner, Fair Play Collection

All inquiries should be made to the Publisher via hello@fairplaypublishing.com.au

NATIONAL LIBRARY OF AUSTRALIA

A catalogue record of this book is available from the National Library of Australia.

This is amazing. It brought back so many great memories. All kids should read this and aspire to be a Matilda or a Socceroo.

John Aloisi

Socceroo and Coach

The Goals That Changed Australia is a captivating journey through the heart of Australian football, weaving together the stories of our Matildas and Socceroos like never before. David Weiner brilliantly captures the passion, resilience, and iconic moments that have defined our game, from John Aloisi's and Cortnee Vine's unforgettable penalties to the incredible highs of the FIFA Women's World Cup. This book is a must read for young fans who dream big and believe in the power of sport to unite a nation. It's an inspiring celebration of Australian football's unique story, destined to ignite pride in the next generation.

Heather Garriock

Matilda and TV Analyst

Childhood is when our earliest - and strongest - memories are formed. With sport (and football especially), big moments can often form lifetime passions. This book captures so many of the big moments that have affected football in Australia over the last twenty years. Many kids will have grown up loving the game because of them. What better reference point for the next generation than this book, which tells those stories in such vivid detail, thanks to David's passion and eye for a story.

Simon Hill

Journalist and Commentator

A comprehensive chronicle, which I am sure fans will appreciate.

Dr Andy Harper

National Soccer League player and TV Analyst

For Cooper and Teya

Contents

Introduction

From John Aloisi to Cortnee Vine, Two Goals that Changed Australia

Forty-two metres.

The loneliest walk in sport, from the halfway line to the penalty spot. Can you imagine it? Fifty-two thousand fans in the stands, all with their eyes on you.

Your teammates' dreams rely on you. Your friends and family hold their breath. Their hearts are racing. Yours is pounding out of your chest. The goalkeeper watches as you stride those 42 metres from the halfway line to the penalty spot.

You, against the goalkeeper. You, against yourself.

On August 12, 2023, you were probably watching a penalty shootout. It was the Matildas against France, the FIFA Women's World Cup quarter-final in Brisbane. Chances are you were, because it was one of the most watched television programs Australia has ever seen, reaching more than seven million Aussies who wanted to see if we would make it to the final four teams of a FIFA World Cup for the first time.

Now imagine you're the *twentieth* kick in that world record World Cup shootout, and it is your turn to make that 42-metre walk.

With all that pressure in mind, 25-year-old Cortnee Vine strode 42 metres, placed the ball on the white spot and struck a goal that created Australian football history.

Ice cool.

This team was *different*.

With the pressure on, they went where no other team in gold had ever gone before.

As the noise in Brisbane's stadium erupted and social media lit up across the country, Vine's life changed forever. She became the face of the Matildas' iconic triumph. This one was extra special: history on home soil, with twenty-three new heroes becoming household names as football fever gripped our country.

The longest penalty shootout in men's or women's World Cup history came after 120 roller-coaster minutes packed with twists and turns.

To those old enough to have lived it, that's what Australian football has been.

A roller coaster packed with twists and turns.

Our story, which reignited and came back to life in another penalty shootout in 2005, when the Socceroos made it to their first World Cup after a 32-year wait.

I took my son to a school fancy dress recently and stood and counted all the kids wearing football kits.

Messi, Miami. Ronaldo, Al-Nassr. Bellingham, Madrid. Mbappe, PSG. Salah, Liverpool. Haaland, City.

The same goes at training, parties, on TV and your phones. They are the names in the games you play and the books you read.

But that collection is missing an amazing story, which took place right here in your own backyard—a story that does not need to be the stuff of fantasy or played out in your imagination. It is a story lived by people just like you—Aussie boys and girls, short and tall, from all corners of the country—who took their dreams and made them real.

They have given us, Australian football fans, a life of highs and lows and everything in between, a roller coaster all of Australia seemed to ride in 2023 during the FIFA Women's World Cup in Australia and New Zealand. Suddenly, there was a new wave of Matildas gold jerseys sprinkled amongst all the colours at the local park as well.

I also can't get enough of Messi, Ronaldo, Bellingham and co. But I love nothing more than the excitement of following our Socceroos and Matildas. They are our teams. And as this story tells, you can take on the world from Down Under. We have some incredible athletes who have done just that.

It hasn't been easy; but football often teaches us about life. There are ups, downs and lessons to be learnt. There are plenty in this story.

I hope, as you read it, you'll feel immense pride in wearing a green and gold kit with your mates, be it a Kerr #20, or Irvine #22. For every teenage sensation like Spain's Lamine Yamal that you follow closely, keep an eye out for our very own, like Nestory Irankunda at Bayern Munich, one of the many talents to come from our local league in Australia, which you can watch week-in, week-out. And for every Zinedine Zidane, Megan Rapinoe or Ronaldo clip you discover on YouTube, you'll find joy in uncovering Mark Viduka, Lisa De Vanna, Harry Kewell and many more.

Viduka and Kewell were the headline acts in 2005 when John Aloisi struck the winning penalty in a shootout that changed Australian football forever.

In 2023 in Brisbane, the baton passed from Aloisi to Cortnee Vine and Australian football went to a place it has never been before.

Everything that has happened to the Matildas and Socceroos before and in between those shootouts is an epic story. I hope you enjoy it.

The Game That Changed Everything

2005 FIFA World Cup Play-Off Second Leg:
Socceroos vs Uruguay

In 2005, billionaire businessman and chairman of Football Australia, Frank Lowy, was fed up. In his grand vision for Australian football, the plan was simple: the Socceroos must be at the World Cup. It was 2005. The last time Australia played in a World Cup, it was 1974! Enough was enough. No more heartbreak.

Frank Lowy didn't build the Westfield shopping empire and become one of Australia's richest men without making big decisions. When he answered an SOS call to take over Australian football and revive the sport, he had plenty of big decisions to make, especially to ensure Australia was at the 2006 World Cup in Germany.

This team had to be there. We had players in England's Premier League, Italy's Serie A, Spain's La Liga, and playing regularly in the UEFA Champions League and UEFA Cup (now known as the Europa League).

But together as the Socceroos, making World Cups had become like a curse and the team was not in good form.

Lowy felt something had to change. He sacked coach Frank Farina, a Socceroos legend, and convinced a Dutch football icon, Guus Hiddink, to come Down Under to manage our national team.

To people like Hiddink, Australia was a land for kangaroos, not footballers! And certainly not for a person with his reputation in the sport. He had won trophies at club level in Holland, but the World Cup was his playground.

He took his country to the semi-finals in 1998. When he took South Korea to the final four in 2002, he was a MIRACLE worker. They even built him a statue afterwards! Hiddink was seen as the missing ingredient. The Socceroos needed some of his genius and luck. Hiddink was inspired and took on the job.

A familiar obstacle lay in Australia's way to making the 2006 World Cup: *Uruguay*, a country with just 3.4 million people but where football is their religion.

They won the first ever World Cup in 1930, and another in 1950. In 2030, to celebrate 100 years of the tournament, FIFA will hold anniversary matches at their famous Estadio Centenario in Montevideo, their capital city.

Their superstar Alvaro Recoba, a wizard-like winger at Inter Milan, even said they had a "divine right to play in the World Cup".

In other words: they belong there, not us.

Four years earlier, they beat the Socceroos at the same play-off stage over two games, extending our World Cup exile to seven tournaments. Australia led 1-0, thanks to Kevin Muscat's penalty at a packed Melbourne Cricket Ground, before Uruguay were simply too good in Montevideo, winning 3-0 in South America to progress 3-1 over both games.

It was a horrible experience.

The moment Australia arrived in Uruguay, it was hostile. Bags were delayed. Fans waited for them, spitting and throwing things. They cursed and hissed, crowding their bus as they tried to leave the airport. "The bus ride was hell," remembered Tony Vidmar. Fireworks were lit at night near the hotel to keep the players awake.

The locals wanted our players to feel as uncomfortable as possible.

To Uruguayans, they had to do everything they could for their team, even if it wasn't exactly great sportsmanship. The whistles throughout the match were deafening. They played their part, and their heroes did the rest on the park.

Dream over, some Socceroos left the field in tears.

Four years later, it was time for revenge. The dirty little tricks wouldn't work this time, and Lowy was leaving no stone unturned to get the country there.

There was just one slight problem…

Hiddink could not believe what he saw in his first games in charge. Even though Australia beat the Solomon Islands 9-1 over two legs, Guus was so angry he was kicking chairs over on the sideline in frustration. He had a lot to do. Quickly.

He wanted to teach his Australians how to play smart football, not just run more than others.

He also made sure Lowy gave him everything he needed.

Even if that meant an aeroplane!

When Uruguay tried their old tricks and wanted to change kick-off times to suit them, a Qantas plane was booked just for the Socceroos to leave straight after full-time of the first leg in Uruguay. Massage tables, physio areas, space to sleep, nutritious food—you name it, the Socceroos had it.

Instead of getting terrible jet lag and sore muscles on the way back, the Socceroos were in luxury. Meanwhile, their rivals were squashed on a normal flight, at a bad time.

Every second counted, even if the advantage was all in the mind.

This time, playing away in the first leg, there were no rude shocks for the Socceroos. They were prepared for a hostile reception in South America.

The green and gold stood strong as 55,000 locals jeered them for 90 minutes. They knew millions of Aussies were waking up early on the morning of November 12 to watch the match live on *SBS*, and that they needed a good result to bring home to Stadium Australia in Sydney.

Hiddink loved Harry Kewell, and he started Australia's superstar despite him battling terrible injuries at Liverpool. With Archie Thompson on the other flank, they worked so hard. The Socceroos defended bravely, led by Tony Popovic and Tony Vidmar. Mark Schwarzer made some big saves.

Dario Rodriguez gave Uruguay a 1-0 victory, but that was a very even position to come home with. The Socceroos were quietly confident.

This time, fans in Sydney would give the South Americans a taste of their own medicine.

"BOOOOOOOOOOOOOOOOOOOOOOOOO!!!"

The Olympic Stadium, in its biggest moment since the 2000 Games, was perfectly golden. When Uruguay's anthem was played, fans yelled like never before.

The Socceroos knew they had 83,000 fans *with* them. Uruguay knew they had 83,000 fans *against* them.

As the teams were announced, fans were shocked. Kewell was on the bench. Tim Cahill started.

It was so loud, so tense.

There was so much at stake and both sides were incredibly anxious to begin with. 28 minutes in, defender Tony Popovic received a yellow card for a whack across Recoba's face. Immediately, *Aussie Guus* played another stunning trick, confusing Uruguay with a change in tactics.

31st minute:
Defender Tony Popovic OFF
Attacker Harry Kewell ON
35th minute:
Australia 1, Uruguay 0: GOAAAAAAALLLLLLLLLL!

In the years since, the night has been remembered for the penalty shootout drama—but you can't forget Mark Bresciano's finish to bring the overall score to 1-1 across both games, sliding his shot into the top corner after some neat build-up and a fortunate Kewell air swing, which helped the ball trickle perfectly into Bresciano's path.

His celebration? Statuesque. Ice cool. Instantly iconic.

No one could get carried away though. The game was way too tight still.

The hosts were playing well and another goal seemed possible. But the 'away goals rule', which is a tiebreaker where the scores are level after both play-off matches, meant Uruguay were still a big risk. If the 'away goals rule' is being used in a match, then if scores are level, the team who scored more goals away from home wins. They came so close when Recoba missed a great chance. So did Richard Morales.

Each miss made us think, *Maybe it will be Australia's night after all ... PLEASE!*

As time ticked by, including 30 minutes of extra-time, anxious fans got the feeling the match would go to the dreaded penalty shootout.

After thirty-two years, Australia's future would come down to the greatest lottery in sport.

Football does not get more stressful: a World Cup spot on the line, a place Australian football desperately needed *now*, and it would be decided via penalties.

Kewell and Neill were perfect from the spot.

Schwarzer gave the stadium a huge boost as he clawed Rodriguez's effort away.

At 2-1 up, Vidmar strode to the spot. Tony Vidmar? Had he ever taken a penalty? Even his family couldn't believe it. Then they braced themselves as he struck it with his non-preferred left foot!

Vidmar, 35, who walked off four years earlier in tears thinking his World Cup dreams were over, nailed his moment.

"He's the hero," screamed *SBS* commentator Craig Foster. "Tony Vidmar's the hero tonight. He's been a COLOSSUS."

All going to plan.

3-2.

The skipper.

Put it away, Dukes, and get us home.

Oh my god.

Gasps.

Eighty-three thousand people, silent.

Viduka missed the goal entirely, throwing his hands in the air in disgust.

Those scarred by the past thirty-two years could picture it all going wrong again.

But this team had other ideas.

Enter Schwarzer.

The big No. 1 goalkeeper stood as still as a statue in the middle of his goal waiting for Marcelo Zalayeta to strike. He pounced to his left, a big glove swatting away the penalty. WHAT. A. SAVE.

"It's as big as we've seen in Australia," cried Foster. "The sort of heart you

Mark Bresciano

need to make World Cups."

It all came down to Aloisi.

He had put penalties away at training the day before. *Trust yourself*, he thought, as he stayed in the zone. It is just a ball. A goal. My left boot.

Australians crossed their fingers, toes and anything else they could find. Some could barely watch.

Thankfully, Aloisi was the calmest man in the country.

His strike was unstoppable.

Then, so was he as he ripped his shirt off and raced down the field in the most famous sprint in Australian football history.

Aloisi played in his garden with his family when he was a kid, just like you.

That night, he took his childhood celebration and shared it with twenty million Australians.

Disbelief and euphoria:
it was a green and gold party
after John Aloisi
scored against Uruguay

It started one mighty party at the stadium, and across the country. The Socceroos wore shirts saying *Never Say Never,* gold confetti rained from the sky and famous Australian songs blasted through the stadium. Hollywood star John Travolta—or Danny from the movie *Grease*—even partied with the Aussies in the dressing room!

This was a moment millions had dreamt of for generations.

November 16 will forever be remembered for Schwarzer's save, and Aloisi's penalty.

But ten minutes before the shootout, the goalkeeper noticed Zeljko Kalac, the other goalkeeper, warming up.

"Am I about to be taken off?" Schwarzer started to think.

Focus. Focus, Mark.

Somehow, he did.

With a decade of experience in European club football under his belt, he knew how to handle tough moments. Fortunately for Schwarzer, Brett Emerton got a cramp in his legs and had to go off, using up the side's last available sub.

Schwarzer's heroics meant one of Australia's finest footballers was now fittingly a national hero for all sports-loving Australians. No Aussie has played more games in the Premier League than the goalkeeper's 514. In fact, he is in the all-time top ten for games played, thanks to stints at Middlesbrough (332 games), Fulham (172), Leicester City (6) and Chelsea (4). He was part of the Leicester (2015) and Chelsea (2016) squads when they won the Premier League, although on the bench at the late stage of his career.

Think about that for a minute. Of all the players in the world who dream of playing in the world's most popular league, an Aussie, who learnt the game at Marconi in Sydney and who left for Germany at 22 to follow his dreams, is in

The most important scoreboard in Australian football history:
Sydney Olympic Park, November 16, 2005

the top ten for most games played. Spots 9, 10 and 11? Local English legends Jamie Carragher, Phil Neville, Steven Gerrard and Rio Ferdinand. That's super impressive, to go with playing more games for Australia than anyone else.

It wasn't the first time he'd saved two penalties in a World Cup shootout, either. In 1993, with long flowing hair and a baby face, he announced himself with heroics against Canada at the Sydney Football Stadium to help Australia progress to a play-off with Argentina, which they ultimately lost.

Aloisi, meanwhile, is the only Australian to score in the 'big three' Euro leagues: Premier League, Serie A and La Liga. He has even scored against Real Madrid at the famous Santiago Bernabeu Stadium. He is another of the Golden Generation who played for his local club (Adelaide City) and then took on the world.

As he waved his jersey over his head, smile beaming, Craig Foster's emotions spilled over in commentary on *SBS*, the television station which championed Australian football when others didn't. They are the true believers.

"Johnnnnny Waaaarrrrennn," he yelled, remembering his old colleague who had passed away in 2004.

It was bittersweet that Australia made the World Cup and our beloved Captain Socceroo was not there to enjoy it.

When most had given up through years in the wilderness, he fought harder for our sport. He always said, one day, Australia would wake up to the power of football, and he'd tell everyone:

I Told You So.

Some fans made a giant banner with those words on that famous night.

November 16, 2005.

The date Australian football changed forever.

Thirty-one years, four months and twenty-four days later, we were no longer in exile. WORLD CUP, HERE WE COME.

You told us so.

The Golden Generation's Golden Moment

2006 FIFA World Cup, Germany

These days, we can get whatever we want, whenever we want, on our phones and devices. Want to see a highlight? Jump on YouTube. You might have even been lucky enough to get a ticket to a World Cup game on home soil in 2023. Recently, we've been spoilt.

So can you imagine waiting thirty-two years for one special football match? That is how long Australia waited for June 12, 2006.

1978 in Argentina.

1982 in Spain.

1986 in Mexico.

1990 in Italy.

1994 in the United States.

1998 in France.

2002 in Japan and South Korea.

Australia was missing.

In 2001, a generation led by the iconic talent of Paul Okon, (the classy midfielder, a star in Belgium, Italy and England, who is now one of Tony Popovic's assistant coaches with the Socceroos) and managed by favourite son Frank Farina (then only 37, who had been an exciting Socceroo striker who played in Belgium, Italy and France) were outgunned by Uruguay for a spot in the 2002 World Cup jointly hosted by South Korea and Japan.

Australia was still a part of the Oceania region at this point. While the rest of the world had a thorough program to qualify, the Socceroos' fate seemed to hang on two huge matches every four years after easing past local rivals.

One of those games from 2001 is now part of football trivia: the world record 31-0 win against American Samoa.

Archie Thompson's 13 goals that day in Coffs Harbour remains a world record for most goals in a competitive international match. The game is so unique it has been featured in a comedy movie, *Next Goal Wins*. But it also summed up that Australia needed more regular, competitive games.

Socceroos 31, American Samoa 0
Archie Thompson: 13 goals
David Zdrilic: 8 goals
Con Boutsianis: 3 goals
Aurelio Vidmar, Tony Popovic, Simon Colosimo: 2 goals
Fausto De Amicis: 1 goal

Craig Foster and Stan Lazaridis after that game at the MCG, November 1997

Missing out in 1997 was brutal. To understand how much our 2005 World Cup qualification meant, you need to understand how close the Socceroos were to making the 1998 France World Cup during an infamous play-off with Iran.

The side brought a 1-1 draw home from Tehran, where 128,000 Iranians made the match as intimidating as possible.

The Socceroos' English boss Terry Venables threw teenager Harry Kewell into that huge match, and he scored a brilliant goal.

At the MCG, a wonderful generation of Socceroos could taste the French croissants, they were that close. Graham Arnold, Robbie Slater, Alex Tobin, Ned Zelic, Mark Bosnich, Aurelio Vidmar. What a group of players.

After 70 minutes, Kewell (again) and Aurelio Vidmar had the hosts 2-0 up.

What happened next was painful. They would not taste the croissants, and many of the veterans would not get another chance to make a World Cup.

A pitch intruder named Peter Hore, known as 'the serial pest', invaded the field, damaged a goal and delayed the game.

When you hear "2-0 is a dangerous lead" from one of your coaches, this is the game they're probably thinking about.

Australia lost focus.

75th minute: Karim Bagheri, 1-2
79th minute: Kohdadad Azizi, 2-2

Four minutes shattered Australian football. Johnny Warren cried on national television. What had just happened?

Bosnich sat slumped on the turf as Azizi celebrated madly.

The goalkeeper, along with Robbie Slater, were the first two Aussie players to win the Premier League, putting Australian footballers on the world map. Slater was with Blackburn as a speedy attacking player. Bosnich was a larger-than-life personality who Sir Alex Ferguson signed from Aston Villa to replace Peter Schmeichel in 1999 at Manchester United. It is remarkable to think that two of the nation's most successful stars never made it to the World Cup stage, but that is the cruel card Australian football was dealt in the 1990s.

That was the one that got away and triggered deep national football wounds.

Four years earlier, in 1993, it was Diego Maradona who stood in Australia's way. One of the world's most famous humans almost single-handedly steered Argentina to the World Cup in the United States.

Over the years, the likes of Kuwait, New Zealand, Scotland—coached by future Manchester United icon Alex Ferguson—and Israel have also provided the final, insurmountable hurdle.

You need to go way back to 1974 for our pioneers, the first Aussies to make the World Cup finals.

Warren was there, part of a team of part-time players who went up against global giants, being one of just sixteen teams to qualify.

Jimmy McKay scored a rocket in a tough play-off against South Korea, earning Australia a place in a group against hosts West Germany, East Germany and Chile.

Peter Wilson with Franz Beckenbauer
before the World Cup match
between West Germany and Australia, 1974

Rale Rasic, an Australian football treasure, was the first man to coach us to a World Cup.

Fourteen of his twenty-two-man team had recently immigrated to our country to get a fresh start in their lives.

They were led by Peter Wilson. Manfred Schaefer was the defensive key and Atti Abonyi and Adrian Alston were the side's best goal threats.

This squad paved the way for football in our country. Players came from clubs like St George Budapest, Hakoah Eastern Suburbs, Club Marconi, Yugal, and Pan Hellenic SC. Our game here was built on the backs of these great clubs.

East Germany (2-0) and West Germany (3-0) were too good, but a historic 0-0 with Chile would be Australia's first World Cup point.

It would be our only point until June 12, 2006.

Eleven thousand, six hundred and seventy-eight days later...

The build-up to the World Cup, ironically also in Germany, was electrifying; it was like counting the days until Christmas, but with a nervous excitement. The anticipation hurt! We knew we had a good team that could surprise the world. But this is the world stage. Make a mistake, and it could be over before you know it.

Rugby league, AFL, cricket—you name it, it had to take a back seat to football in June 2006, as front and back pages of newspapers were filled with news out of Germany.

June 2006 opened Australia's eyes to how big the football world is. How can you be taken seriously as a sporting nation until you're back on the greatest stage of all? So used to being the best in smaller sports, the Australian audience got a glimpse of football in all its glory: an incredible atmosphere in Germany, a carnival with fans from every country on Earth, the biggest stars from every continent in one place and a competition that stopped the world.

And we were part of it. Welcome back, Australia.

It was a magical time.

To make it even more special, Australia was drawn against royalty: world champions Brazil, featuring Ronaldo, Ronaldinho, Roberto Carlos, Cafu; some of the greatest players to ever live.

But first, Japan. If Hiddink's side had any dreams of progressing, they had to take points out of the first game. This was the final tournament Australia would contest representing Oceania before moving into the Asian region, so they were drawn against an Asian opponent who would go on to become one of our most regular rivals in the years to come. (In World Cups, teams from the same region cannot be drawn in the same group.)

On a glorious sunny day in Kaiserslautern, the Socceroos could not believe what they saw as the team bus made its way to the venue.

Australians were out in force; the German city had turned gold.

Hiddink sprang some major surprises. Tim Cahill was on the bench. Bristol City's Luke Wilkshire was a bolter in the first team; Hiddink saw a quality in the hard-working Wollongong local and handed him an opportunity that changed his career. From an unknown, he took his chance and became one of the first Aussies picked from then on.

Australia had options; this was a Golden Generation of players unlike anything we've assembled since.

Australia's first World Cup lineup in three decades was stacked with European talent, with six Premier League stars: Mark Schwarzer (Middlesbrough), Lucas Neill (Blackburn), Craig Moore (Newcastle), Brett Emerton (Blackburn), Harry Kewell (Liverpool) and Mark Viduka (Middlesbrough), plus Jason Culina (PSV Eindhoven), Scott Chipperfield (Basel) and Italian club Parma's Vince Grella and Mark Bresciano.

It was a period full of so much talent we probably took that depth for granted. Take, for example, Emerton. If he was in today's generation, he would be one of the headline acts. When Kewell was flying down the left, Emerton held the right together ninety-seven times. His journey is one of note for youngsters, because he was patient. He went to Europe with nearly one hundred games in Australia under his belt. He was ready to go. He won the UEFA Cup (now Europa League) with Dutch club Feyenoord before playing week in, week out with Blackburn across eight years in the Premier League.

The bench was also elite.

Cahill was one of Everton's main men, and Tony Popovic (Crystal Palace), Josip Skoko (Wigan) and Stan Lazaridis (Birmingham) all played in England.

Zeljko Kalac was at AC Milan. Across Europe, Josh Kennedy was in Germany, Mile Sterjovski in Switzerland and John Aloisi was scoring in La Liga for Alaves in Spain. Two players were from the A-League: future captain Mark Milligan, and defender Michael Beauchamp. Sadly, play-off hero Tony Vidmar had to withdraw from the squad after doctors noticed a heart condition.

Central defender Popovic would go on to become the first member of this group to *coach* the Socceroos, appointed in September 2024 to lead his country's quest to the 2026 World Cup in America, Canada and Mexico. A tough, smart and skilful defender, Popovic's leadership qualities were always clear. He was made captain of his beloved Sydney United at 20 years of age and also led English outfit Crystal Palace. He wore the green and gold 58 times during a top class Socceroos career, where one of the highlights was the night he scored one of the three goals in Australia's iconic 3-1 win over a star studded England in a 2003 friendly, a game where Wayne Rooney made his international debut and the opposition was captained by David Beckham (Emerton and Kewell scored the other two goals).

There are few records in Australian football quite like his. He has played at World Cups for the under-17s, under-20s and Socceroos, as well as the Olympics. As a coach, he works his players hard and expects the best, has improved many players and has had an outstanding career in Australia. He has won A-League Premierships with Western Sydney and Perth Glory, an Australia Cup with Melbourne Victory, made five Grand Finals and most remarkably, is the only Australian to coach a side to an Asian Champions League trophy. That came in 2014 with Western Sydney, crowned the best club side in Asia just two years into their existence after a gripping 1-0 win over two games against Saudi Arabia powerhouse Al-Hilal. It earned him the title of Asia's coach of the year.

When he accepted the Socceroos job in September 2024, he beamed: "the dream job can come true".

The green and gold jersey means the world to him and his *Golden Generation*.

"We always wore that shirt with integrity, and we wore it as a privilege, as a badge of honour," he explained.

Popovic was one of many leaders in 2006, but the side was captained by

Viduka. To many, the striker is the most gifted player the nation has ever produced. Hiddink knew he needed him fit and firing, so he made him captain: he wanted him to know he was the main man.

Mark Viduka was a product of Melbourne Knights, a club with a proud Croatian tradition. He won the Johnny Warren Medal for NSL Player of the Year, Young Player of the Year and Top Scorer in 1993/4 and 1994/5—while in his teens. He was so impressive that the Croatian president personally tried to persuade him to join Dinamo Zagreb.

Viduka was not the fastest; he certainly wasn't the fittest. He just had a pure mastery of the ball, and when he was on, he scored goals for fun wherever he played. Dinamo Zagreb. Celtic. Leeds. Middlesbrough. Newcastle United. He regularly finished in the top five on the Premier League scorer's charts, is a member of the Sport Australia Hall of Fame, and is best remembered for the day he beat Liverpool all on his own, scoring four times for Leeds in a 4-3 win.

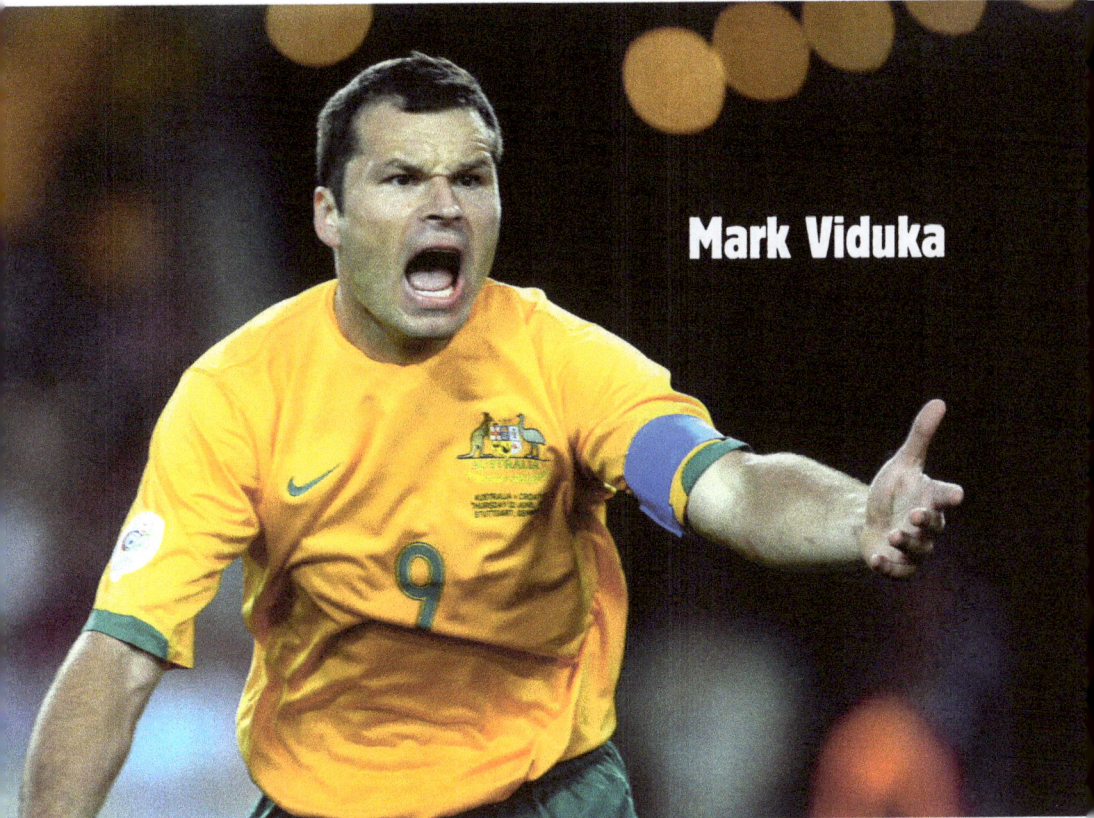

Mark Viduka

When the Premier League's all-time top scorer Alan Shearer signed Viduka while coaching Newcastle, he took one look at him at training and phoned his friend, Michael Bridges, telling him, "I've never seen a talent quite like this guy!"

Hiddink had put Viduka, and the entire squad, through a gruelling preparation for the World Cup.

They were super fit, as you'd expect from Aussies.

But the Dutchman also added game smarts.

They were ready.

This was it.

We rose for the national anthem, tears in our eyes, hands on hearts.

And then, damn it. 0-1.

Shunsuke Nakamura sailed a 26th-minute free-kick towards goal, which floated over everyone's head and into the net. Australia protested that Schwarzer had been fouled. It did not matter.

Socceroos fans slumped. Thirty-two years, for this! The players were made of sterner stuff, though. They settled into the game. On a brutally hot day, they were fitter than the Japanese. Momentum turned.

Hiddink also had a trick up his sleeve.

Tim Cahill. Super sub.

Fuming at being left out of the first team, the 26-year-old had a point to prove.

He arrived eight minutes into the second-half as the Socceroos started to pound Japan's goal looking for an equaliser.

Time ticked by. How had we not scored?! We were worried. Hiddink unleashed Aloisi and Kennedy. Just as Australia's World Cup looked over before it even got going …

84 minutes: 1-1
89 minutes: 2-1
90 minutes: 3-1

"CAHILL. CAAAAHIIIIIL. TIM CAHILL HAS DONE IT AGAIN! WHAT A GOAL BY TIM CAHILL," screamed Simon Hill in a famous piece of commentary.

"OH, IT'S A WONDERFUL MOMENT IN KAISERSLAUTERN."

Euphoria. Joy. Relief.

THIS is what the World Cup is all about.

The country erupted. Socceroos fans sung Aussie songs in the stadium. A nation had caught the football bug.

Cahill scored the nation's first ever FIFA World Cup men's goal with a brilliant poacher's finish; he grabbed the three points with a daring, brave shot from outside the box. Aloisi surged through to put the icing on the cake. The penalty hero calls this goal the most cherished of his career. *A World Cup goal.*

It was now very real. Australia had its first win.

Those six minutes were watched over, and over, and over again. The country was very tired that morning. Australia was celebrating three World Cup points for the very first time.

Next up, though.

Gulp. Take a look at those clubs!

BRAZIL

DIDA
(AC Milan)

ROBERTO
CARLOS
(Real Madrid)

CAFU
(AC Milan)

LUCIO
(Bayern)

JUAN
(Bayer Leverkusen)

EMERSON
(Juventus)

ZE ROBERTO
(Bayern)

KAKA
(AC Milan)

ADRIANO
(Inter Milan)

RONALDO
(Real Madrid)

RONALDINHO
(Barcelona)

To fans in 2024, Brazil is Neymar, Alisson and Vinicius Junior. Twenty years ago though, the *Selecao* were the ultimate football team. They won the World Cup in 1994 and 2002, and they were in the final in 1998. This was a side you

played against in video games, not in real life. Fantasy football. Ronaldo, Cafu and Roberto Carlos would feature in many fans' all-time world team.

This match is what dreams are made of.

The history books might show a 2-0 defeat for Australia, but it was one of the nation's most accomplished performances in front of the world's eyes.

The Brazilians needed until the second-half to break the game open; goals to Adriano and Fred put the brave Aussies away.

The Australians were not just gutsy underdogs. They surprised the world with their football quality. At 0-1, there were some glorious chances to draw level, particularly for Kewell.

Everyone was extremely proud of the performance but focus had to quickly shift to a Group F 'grand final' against Croatia.

Can you believe Australia was drawn to face Croatia? Football has an uncanny way of providing drama you cannot make up if you tried.

A Croatia side featuring three players *born* in Australia took on a Socceroos side with seven players of Croatian heritage.

Josip Simunic, Joey Didulica and Anthony Seric opted to play for Croatia, while Mark Viduka, Zeljko Kalac, Josip Skoko, Tony Popovic, Jason Culina, Ante Covic and Mark Bresciano all had family ties to their opponents.

There were some families who did not know which team to support!

The matchup was fitting. The Socceroos were a proud squad of Australians coming from many different backgrounds. This Golden Generation was built and inspired by families who moved to Australia from Europe. The impact of those communities, including Croatia with clubs like Sydney United and Melbourne Knights, has been huge, just as football in Australia has been a big part of their lives.

Five of those players started in Stuttgart, and in a stunning move, one of them was Kalac, with Hiddink dropping Schwarzer.

That didn't go well.

Darijo Srna scored a special free-kick for Croatia after just two minutes; Craig Moore slotted a penalty just before half-time after a silly handball in the box to level the scores.

The second-half EXPLODED. It was wild.

Kalac let a tame shot trickle past him. At 2-1 down, the Socceroos were heading out. A draw would be enough to progress, but an equaliser was needed to earn that precious point.

ON: Aloisi

ON: Kennedy

ON: Bresciano

Hiddink was prepared to gamble, and by now, had *eight* attacking players on.

Sport might be unpredictable, but sometimes, it provides the perfect story.

Just as it looked like Croatia might hold on, Bresciano floated a left-foot cross that sailed to the left of the box where Kewell waited.

Kewell's finish was a cool one. He flicked the ball with his left foot, thumped it with his right and was sprinting downfield in sheer happiness the moment it left his boot.

The pin-up boy had done it!

The golden boy of the Golden Generation scored the golden goal that would send Australia into the World Cup knockout phase.

But first, the drama wasn't over.

It was heaving on the field. Emotions were running high. Croatia were desperate. Australia were hanging on. Even the referee lost his mind!

In one of the most comical moments ever at a World Cup, English referee Graham Poll gave Simunic THREE YELLOW CARDS. Somehow, he forgot to send him off after two.

Amid the mayhem, he sent Emerton off for a harsh handball, and Aloisi seemingly scored to clinch victory, but Poll blew full-time instead.

When he did, we all took a massive deep breath. Not only to believe what just happened, but to comprehend what the side had achieved.

Spain, France, Brazil, Ghana, Switzerland, Ukraine, Italy, Portugal, the Netherlands, England, Ecuador, Germany, Sweden, Argentina and Mexico were all in the last 16.

So too, Australia.

After thirty-two years out of the tournament, that was one mighty group to be a part of.

Moore's goal was a reward for his persistence fighting injuries. A legend at Scottish club Rangers, who scouted him straight from the 1993 FIFA Youth World Cup in Australia, he was actually the Socceroos captain but had to miss the Uruguay series through injury. With no television coverage in England, his old pal Kevin Muscat had to commentate the shootout over the phone for him! After signing for Premier League club Newcastle in July 2005, he battled a hamstring injury that kept him out until March. He returned and would not be denied his place in the side's defence or the Socceroos' epic story.

Kewell was the fitting hero that night, the superstar in an era full of amazing talent.

It is hard not to think *what if* when it comes to Kewell, a wizard from Smithfield in Sydney's west who made his debut for Leeds United at 17, producing a highlight reel from left wing as good as anyone in the league at the time. He made the PFA Premier League team of the year in 1999-2000 and alongside Viduka, steered Leeds to the UEFA Champions League semis in 2001. As a duo, they made Leeds popular in Australia. He had rock-star looks and delivered on the park.

The secret to such a freakish talent coming out of Australia? Thousands and thousands of repetitions, according to Kewell, who once explained, "As far back as I can remember, I was always kicking a ball around. Coming from Australia I was exposed to a lot of other sports, everything from rugby league, tennis, golf—anything that requires hand-eye coordination or an ability to run."

Leeds fans were gutted when Kewell moved to Liverpool in 2003 at the peak of his powers after being courted by all the world's biggest clubs. He won a Champions League and FA Cup at the Reds but battled badly with injury. Kewell worked so hard in the gym, but dreaded injuries kept popping up at the wrong time.

One of those was midway through the 2006 FA Cup final. When he hobbled off, Socceroos' fans held their breath. He was now racing the clock for Germany.

Ever the professional, Kewell trained the house down and produced a brilliant World Cup. But after the jubilation of his historic goal against Croatia, his body let him down again. Socceroos fans couldn't believe it when he walked out in the Round of 16 using crutches.

After Croatia's emotional roller coaster, the Socceroos' next rival was no stranger to many Aussie fans.

The Azzurri.

Italy is a nation with such deep links for so many football-loving Aussies. Lots of families grew up supporting Italy; Serie A is incredibly popular. We had clubs across the country built by Italian migrants that shaped our game, like APIA Leichhardt, Marconi Stallions, Adelaide City, Brunswick Zebras and Brisbane City. Lygon Street in Melbourne and Norton Street in Sydney, both hotbeds of Italian life, had the night of nights when the match was held.

The Italian team in Germany was simply remarkable. Take the time and watch highlights of Andrea Pirlo, Alessandro Del Piero (who also played with Sydney FC!) and Francesco Totti. They are all-time icons. Many would say Gianluigi Buffon was the best goalkeeper ever, and Fabio Cannavaro, the captain, was the greatest defender of the modern era.

Back in Kaiserslautern with World Cup fever now truly gripping everyone back home, our Aussies had the Italians on the ropes. Our team played against elite stars every week for their clubs; they did not look out of place or show fear on this big stage. For 94 stressful minutes, it remained scoreless, even after Marco Materazzi was sent off with 40 minutes left for a late lunge as Mark Bresciano ran towards goal.

The Socceroos were going toe-to-toe with Italy. Gigi Buffon had to save a strong Scott Chipperfield shot, but the green and gold could not create any more chances despite having an extra player.

Hiddink had kept fresh subs on the bench to run over Italy in extra-time but FIVE MINUTES into stoppage-time, disaster struck.

It is a moment that still haunts, and divides, Australian football fans. Seconds before the game would have gone into extra-time, Fabio Grosso galloped into the box.

Lucas Neill—who was so good at the World Cup there were rumours Barcelona wanted him—lunged desperately, and probably needlessly. Grosso needed no invitation. He went down.

PENALTY.

We all felt sick.

Was it a dive? Was it bad defending? It didn't matter.

Totti hammered his penalty past Schwarzer. There was no time left. It was the last kick of the game. Suddenly, the dream was over.

This is football. No movie you'll ever see is as unpredictable.

In 2006, Australia was given a taste of something very, very special.

The Socceroos' performance looked even more impressive when Italy subsequently won that World Cup. The final against France, won in a penalty shootout, is best known for Zinedine Zidane head-butting Materazzi, in Zidane's final game of professional football.

Guus Hiddink left as Aussie Guus and a national hero.

Kewell. Viduka. Schwarzer. Cahill. Aloisi. They were now names everyone knew. Football was back, and with a new local league gaining momentum, this was everything Aussie football fans had ever wanted.

After the World Cup, the Socceroos were a box-office ticket, touring the country playing Asian Cup and World Cup qualifiers.

From 2006, Australia moved out of Oceania into Asia, a move long recommended for several reasons.

Until 2026, Oceania never had a guaranteed World Cup spot. Moving to Asia helped get away from the lottery of those brutal play-offs to a fairer path to the World Cup; plus, Australia needed to play more competitive football, more regularly.

It also meant Australia was invited to the Asian Cup every four years.

However, our first appearance did not end well, ending the World Cup honeymoon.

Graham Arnold, Hiddink's assistant, took charge and the superstars struggled badly in the heat in Indonesia, Thailand and Malaysia. Fresh off the World Cup, the Socceroos underestimated how hard the Asian Cup would be. Japan got revenge for 2006, knocking the side out in a quarter-final penalty shootout.

We learnt, straight away, to show more respect to Asian football.

Never Say Die Is Born: Australia's First World Cup Win and First Trophy

2007 FIFA Women's World Cup, China

When a group of women represented Australia for the first time in an international competition in Asia in 1975, they went from pub to pub and held lamington drives to raise money for their tour. When the youngest member of that team, Julie Dolan, was named Australia's women's captain four years later at 18 years of age, she had to hand out leaflets to locals to let them know about their upcoming international against New Zealand at Seymour Shaw Park in Sydney's south.

As she was growing up and trying to play, her best chance of getting a game was with the boys at school.

If you love Sam Kerr, Mary Fowler, Katrina Gorry or Mackenzie Arnold, there are some other legendary ladies you need to get to know. They made it possible for us to sit with 83,000 fans in a packed football stadium to see the Matildas today.

If they'd been playing today, they'd be the household heroes.

They're the pioneers.

While the Socceroos were in the World Cup wilderness, our unsung Matildas were already on the world stage, making World Cups in 1995, 1999 and 2003, plus the 2000 and 2004 Olympic Games.

In 1995 the 'Matildas' nickname was born—finally changing from the Female Socceroos.

Fun Fact: The Matildas' name came from a competition run by *SBS*. The national team, now widely and affectionately known as the Matildas—or the Tillies—was inspired by the iconic song 'Waltzing Matilda'.

They might have been on the world stage, but there was a long way to go to get the attention and conditions they deserved. For many, it cost more to play for Australia than they earned for it; some lost jobs as a result of their time away.

The 1975 Australian women's team
who played in the first
Women's Asian Championship in Hong Kong

"I went to a World Cup and then back to school with nothing," remembered Julie Murray, the captain in 1995, talking to *Code Sports.*

But their love of their country, sport and teammates meant they did not give up.

Now, our stars call London, Manchester and Paris home; then, this group didn't even have a national league in Australia at one point. They battled on to make it possible for this wave of players, and for you, to turn dreams into reality.

A Julie Murray goal against New Zealand in Papua New Guinea qualified the side for their first ever World Cup in 1995 in Sweden, where she was also the captain.

Qualifying sparked great celebrations for the squad, but the tournament itself was a real learning curve. A group who had to largely train by themselves prior to the tournament copped 13 goals against powerhouses Denmark, China and USA. But there were memorable moments. Angela Iannotta and Sunni Hughes made China work for their win, while Lisa Casagrande's super header saw the side 1-0 up against the USA with 20 minutes to go.

The existence of a World Cup caught the attention of future Matildas, and with the Sydney Olympics on the horizon, there was quite a bit to play for. In the United States, 1999 was a tasty look into the future, with millions of fans and eyeballs on the tournament. The 91,185 fans at the final, where Brandi Chastain did something no one had ever done before and famously whipped her shirt off in an excited frenzy after scoring the winning penalty, remained a world record for women's football until 2022.

There was a first point for Australia thanks to Julie Murray's goal against Ghana (Murray made the tournament's All Star team as well) but perhaps the most infamous moment from 1999 came via teenager Alicia Ferguson. 'Eesh', a Matildas legend who was the side's Head of Delegation in 2023, provides a brilliant example in dealing with adversity in your football—or life —journey.

Then just 17, she was so fired up for her World Cup debut in the final group game against China that she flew into a tackle and her match lasted ... 95 seconds. In what remains a world record red card, she was marched for a late tackle that left her in tears.

Years later, she can laugh at it. Importantly, at the time, she used the low to reshape her career, to not let herself get overwhelmed by the moment.

"I had two choices: I could let it bother me, or I could just crack on and get on with it," she told the *ABC* in 2023.

"People make mistakes, but it's how you react to them, isn't it?

"I found the positive in that experience. It was horrible at the time, but it actually made me a more mature player and a better player in the long run, because it changed my whole mentality and approach."

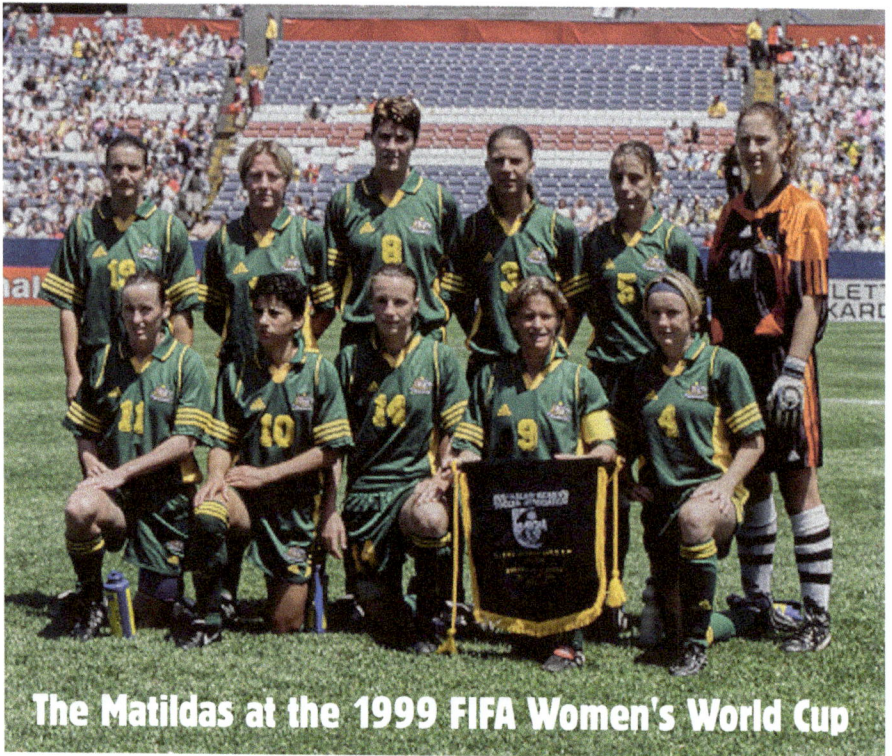

The Matildas at the 1999 FIFA Women's World Cup

The Matildas' pursuit of a first win would have to wait until 2003, a World Cup that was quickly moved to USA from China at the last minute. The side finished bottom of a group with Russia, China and Ghana, but Kelly Golebiowski had the side 1-0 up against Russia, while Heather Garriock had given her side an early lead against the Chinese, and also scored against Ghana.

It really was a different time. Tal Karp retired at 23 after the 2003 tournament to concentrate on her law degree. There was such little exposure or media around the side that players like Pam Bignold snuck cameras into games to document their journeys.

In 2005, the Socceroos got their own plane to return for the home leg of their World Cup qualifier against Uruguay.

In 2005, the Matildas were still paying for their own laundry when away on tour.

As the Socceroos dominated headlines, the Matildas lived in a different world. By the 2007 Women's World Cup, a Matildas' to-do list looked very different to a Socceroos' schedule.

- Training and matches
- Work
- Study
- Wear hand-me-down men's jerseys
- Need to fight for the basics: washing, internet access while in camp, secure contracts
- Take on the world as semi-professional players

On the park, the 2007 World Cup is one of the unsung stories in Australian sport.

Just like the celebrated Socceroos, the Matildas got out of their World Cup group, along with Norway. Canada and Ghana were eliminated.

Tom Sermanni, the wise mentor in charge, helped put the Matildas on the map. In fact, at the time the final touches to this book were made in November 2024, Sermanni was back in charge of the Matildas on a temporary basis while Football Australia searches for a new coach.

Ever heard recently departed Matildas coach Tony Gustavsson talk about his *Never Say Die* Matildas? Well, it's in the team's DNA, formed in the pioneering era.

The group stage came down to a pulsating finish, after the Matildas had four points from the opening two games.

De Vanna was the goal-scoring hero in the first match.

She scored a brace as the country enjoyed our first ever Women's World Cup win, a 4-1 triumph over Ghana. It also featured a fine finish from Sarah Walsh and a clever header from Heather Garriock off Di Alagich's cross.

De Vanna scored the crucial goal in a 1-1 draw with Norway in the second game.

Against Canada, we witnessed a moment anyone watching will never forget.

Canada were leading the Aussies 2-1 after Christine Sinclair scored one of her world record 190 international goals with five minutes left on the clock. If scores remained, the Matildas would be knocked out.

Two icons were not going to let Australia go home. They combined in a goal for the ages.

1. De Vanna, again. Incredible skill down the left of the box to bamboozle three defenders with her touch, and swerve.

2. Salisbury, the skipper. With seven red shirts in the box, she collected De Vanna's perfect pass and calmly slotted the key goal home. She was the central defender—what was she doing there?! Who cares, it was remarkable.

The 33-year-old Salisbury, in her fourth World Cup, and her 138th cap, was drowned by all her teammates jumping on her in celebration. It was the biggest goal in Matildas' history at that point in time.

The time on the clock? 90 + 2 minutes.

INCREDIBLE.

Like Kewell for the Socceroos in 2006, Salisbury was the perfect goal scorer for this special moment.

Australian football needed Cheryl Salisbury in those years. The scorer of our first ever Olympic goal in 2000, she was also one of the first to play in America. She defines the word *trailblazer*. She proved what Australian footballers are capable of.

But the times were so different; she had to work in a chicken factory to pay her way over there.

No one deserved that goal more than Salisbury, the captain since 2003, and the powerful defender from Newcastle, who always stood up for the Matildas and female football. Sometimes her national team duties even came at her own expense financially and physically. But she continued to lead the way, driven by her belief.

She championed female football at a time not everyone listened in an era full of unsung heroes.

You'll read a bit about Brazil in these pages. They became very familiar foes for our Matildas.

In 2007, the South Americans were the powerhouse, and played like it as they took a 2-0 lead in the World Cup quarter-final.

You couldn't keep Lisa De Vanna quiet for long though, and she pounced on a mistake to fire her side back to life with a goal. A semi-final spot was within reach when Lauren Colthorpe headed Heather Garriock's cross to make it 2-2.

Never. Say. Die.

The Matildas' spirit helped them fight back against Brazil. That was some effort, because the South Americans traded their brilliance for brute force that day to try to rattle the Aussies.

But when they needed it, Brazil found their *Braziliance.* Locked at 2-2, Cristiane's long bomb gave them the win that put them into the final four.

That Brazil side was iconic, but our 2007 Matildas took them to the wire at a time when they did not even have a national league back home.

No obstacle was too much for these brilliant footballers, a group who still dominate the all-time leader board for Matildas' appearances.

Clare Polkinghorne, from the current era, leads the way, followed by Salisbury (151), De Vanna (150) and Garriock (130).

From their pioneering leadership, the W-League was born in 2008, paving the way for today's current stars to break into the national team.

Can you imagine how legends from that era feel now? How players like Garriock or Amy Duggan, now television experts, must feel when they work on some of the most watched TV broadcasts ever? In their playing days, many games weren't even on TV. Sarah Walsh, the side's speedy striker, now holds key roles leading female football and planning for its future at Football Australia. How does she feel about the incredible change?

"I think I will never not be shocked to see the Matildas up on outdoor media," she told the *Sydney Morning Herald.*

"(It) never entered my mind when I was playing. So it's important that visibility, in mainstream."

As they started their careers, they were given old Socceroos' kits, were not paid appropriately and even after making World Cups, they had to try publicity stunts to get people's attention.

Now, the Matildas are box-office and it is hard to get a ticket!

For eight years, the Matildas were coached by Tom Sermanni; such was his standing in the sport, his next job in 2012 was with none other than the powerhouse of women's football: the US national team.

Known for the way he treated his players, Matildas of that era speak glowingly of their old coach. He has made a worldwide impact too, also coaching New Zealand and Canada.

Seeds were planted for his Matildas' bright future when they made the 2006 Asian Cup final in their first attempt. That's when *belief* in Asia and beyond really clicked. They made the decider in Adelaide, losing to China in a penalty shootout after Caitlin Munoz and Joey Peters' goals in a 2-2 draw.

By the next Asian Cup in 2010, the group was a perfect mix of experience and youth.

On May 30, the Matildas claimed the country's first senior trophy since moving into Asia.

This was remarkable, and five years before the Socceroos did it.

Japan, China and DPR Korea were the usual big-hitters in this tournament, and by beating DPR Korea in the final, the Matildas also qualified for the next World Cup in 2011. They had to deal with different conditions in China, but the young kids who came in to replace the retired legends of 2007 proved they had something very special about them.

Superstars now, babies then.

We didn't know it at the time, but this trophy hinted that a Golden Generation was coming. Thanks to Sermanni who gave them a go, a talented group of kids were unleashed and proved they were fearless.

Sam Kerr, 16
Kyah Simon, 18
Clare Polkinghorne, 21
Aivi Luik, 25
Elise Kellond-Knight, 19
Lydia Williams, 22
Tameka Butt (Yallop), 18

Does that list look familiar? They were mentored alongside Melissa Barbieri, Heather Garriock, Collete McCallum, Sally Shipard, Kim Carroll, Thea Slatyer, Lauren Colthorpe and Kate Gill, Asia's player of the year in 2010.

Sally Shipard, who made her debut at 16, was now a mainstay, but her move from Wagga Wagga to Sydney as a teenager proved to this group of youngsters, who she was now welcoming, that it was possible. Shipard was a Matildas favourite, who championed mental health and the LGBTQIA+ community long before it became as common as it is today to talk about.

Leena Khamis' header and Kylie Ledbrook's penalty helped open the tournament with a 2-0 win over Vietnam; Kim Carroll, De Vanna and Kerr then sealed a 3-1 result against South Korea, before a 1-0 defeat to China, in the final group game, set up a semi-final against Japan.

Kate Gill, who has gone on to lead the country's Players Association, was the hero in Chengdu. Her unreal long-range finish cashed in on chaos caused by a dangerous delivery from Servet Uzunlar and sealed a 1-0 win and the Matildas' spot in the final.

Guess who opened the scoring in the final? Thirteen years before she was Australia's most famous athlete, a teenage Sam Kerr calmly slotted Polkinghorne's through ball for a 19th-minute lead.

Throughout, Barbieri had been vital in goal. The goalkeeper is one of the true survivors of Australian football. At the 2010 Asian Cup, the 30-year-old was at the heart of this 'Tillies' era. Fourteen years later, at 44, she is still playing! In fact, she started in goal for Melbourne City in the A-League

Women's Grand Final in 2024. That's incredible for someone whose Matildas debut was way back in 2002, after only two years playing as a goalkeeper!

In the 2010 Asian Cup final, she had done all she could to keep out the No. 1-ranked side in the region, but Australia finally conceded in the 73rd-minute, and a tense match went all the way to the penalty spot.

With Sermanni as cool as ever, he handed the decisive final penalty to 18-year-old Kyah Simon.

Her teammates Shiphard, Ledbrook, Gill and Garriock were superb from the spot. When Simon hit the top right corner, it was party time!

"It is a sea of joy by the Matildas," *ABC* commentator Peter Wilkins described joyously.

Sermanni hailed it as the best moment of his career. Before the shootout, his style was to be calm and relaxed.

"Hurry up and get it over with," it is said that he told the team. "'Cos dinner is waiting at the hotel!"

With five perfect penalties, his players also looked confident at the most important moment.

Later, he said, "I couldn't be prouder of this group of girls."

Polkinghorne was part of that group, like she has been throughout the highs and lows of the modern Matildas story.

Unassuming, quiet and humble, she has gone beyond her own heroes since: no one has played more for Australia than she has.

"Clare Polkinghorne is a legend in this game, and will be so for a very, very long time," former Matildas coach, Tony Gustavsson, said of the defender in 2023.

"The way she has carried herself in this team, in this game, for so long, and what she has brought to the team and the game—I can't explain that in words. She is, and always will be, a true legend."

Dedicated and tough, there is one anecdote that sums up the Queenslander's attitude.

She was told to 'man mark' US legend Abby Wambach in a 2008 game. In other words, to follow Wambach *everywhere* on the field.

So, when the American went to the sideline to get some water, so did Polkinghorne!

It sums up a team player and her work ethic. She is an incredible role model for any aspiring footballer.

"I was never the most skilful or talented footballer, but I was definitely one of the hardest-working players in my younger years," she told Football Australia's media.

"I had that discipline, competitiveness and winning mentality to never give up. That is what really set up the rest of my career."

Honour Roll

First World Cup goal: Angela Iannotta, 4-2 loss to China, 1995

First World Cup point: 1-1 v Ghana, 1999. Goal: Alison Forman

First World Cup win: 4-1 v Ghana, 2007. Goals: Lisa De Vanna 2, Heather Garriock, Sarah Walsh

First referee to officiate a World Cup final: Tammy Ogston, 2007 World Cup final

First major international trophy: 2010 AFC Asian Cup, 5-4 in a penalty shootout v DPR Korea in China

Four Points, a New Hero, but an African Sunset for Our Golden Generation

2010 FIFA World Cup, South Africa

After Aussie Guus, Football Australia tried to find Guus 2.0.

Pim Verbeek, another Dutchman, guided the experienced Australians through their first ever World Cup quest in Asia.

The stress of the play-offs were gone; in a league table format, the Socceroos sealed a spot in South Africa with a minimum of fuss against the likes of Qatar, Iraq, China, Bahrain, Uzbekistan and Japan.

Maybe the public found that a bit too easy after years of tension. The performance in 2010 is rarely spoken in the same tones as four years earlier, even though the side once again secured four points in their World Cup group.

This time, however, they did not qualify for the next phase, with Germany and Ghana progressing. Serbia and the Socceroos were eliminated.

Another reason for less celebration was the opening game where Germany spanked the Socceroos 4-0 in Durban. It was an awful night. That Germany side was sublime, so good that they also put four goals past Argentina and England, with the score 4-1 in both games.

However, what made Socceroos fans sad was the way the side was set up to play. In 2006, the green and gold were brave and backed themselves. In Durban, Verbeek sent his side out to defend, and did not even pick a striker.

Pim Verbeek with captain, Lucas Neill

Not having belief that you can win is not the Australian way, and it backfired.

There were thousands of Aussies at the first World Cup to be held on the African continent. If their headache wasn't big enough from the piercing sound of the vuvuzelas (a local instrument that sounds like a car horn!), it was splitting as Lukas Podolski, Miroslav Klose, Thomas Muller and Cacau piled on the pain in their 4-0 loss to Germany.

The tournament was also a sad end to Harry Kewell as a World Cup Socceroo; the injury-plagued legend spent just 24 minutes on the park, not selected against Germany, before being sent off against Ghana for a handball on the goal line.

Thankfully, we saw more of the Australian spirit and ability against the African side, with the side snaring a draw despite playing 66 minutes with ten men. Asamoah Gyan converted the penalty after Kewell's red card to make it 1-1.

Stars everywhere as the Socceroos prepare for their 2010 World Cup clash against Ghana.

Brett Holman was the scorer that day, a reward for the 26-year-old attacker from Dutch club AZ. He came to the World Cup fresh off winning the championship in Holland. Holman's incredible tournament is a lesson in resilience for any young player. First, at club level, he stuck it out in Holland when game time wasn't coming his way after moving from Sydney in 2002. Then, he ignored criticism of his international form to go on to become a fine Socceroo, one who played for ten years in Holland and tasted the Champions League. He had a brilliant World Cup.

Despite the opening loss, Australia went to Nelspruit to face Serbia with the tournament alive as Group D reached a thrilling climax. If you haven't seen the goals from this game, you need to check them out on YouTube— they are quality.

Everyone remembers the Japan triumph in 2006, but this win has fallen under the radar. It shouldn't. They were up against a really strong European

Richard Garcia (left), **Brett Holman** and **Tim Cahill** (centre) and **Jason Culina** (right) after the victory against Serbia

side, including Manchester United rock Nemanja Vidic, and future A-League legend Milos Ninkovic.

Cahill, back after a red card against Germany and suspension, brought his trademark leap, header and corner flag destruction to South Africa. His jump and timing to connect with Luke Wilkshire's cross to open the scoring was Cristiano Ronaldo-esque.

Then Holman, the breakout star of the tournament for the Aussies, picked the ball up from just inside his own half and drove downfield, unleashing a sizzling strike from miles out. A world-class goal on the world stage.

"My old man always said to me, 'have a go'," he told *SBS* years later.

Have a go, he did. Seize the moment when you get your chance.

Progress was still a chance in a chaotic clash. Josh Kennedy and Jason Culina had late chances. But when Mesut Ozil blasted Germany to a 1-0 win over Ghana in a match played at the same time, and Serbia scored to make it 2-1, it was all over for the Socceroos.

A tournament that started so grimly at least ended with Australia's second World Cup win, something we grew to appreciate more as time went on.

Little did we know it would be twelve years until our next World Cup win.

This extraordinary generation had left their mark, changed the sport, provided us with beautiful memories and made the game better for future players.

But was their time up?

Baby-Faced Legends

2011 FIFA Women's World Cup, Germany

The Matildas' 2011 squad is like looking back at an old school photo.

There's a baby-faced Kerr, Simon, Foord, Williams, Yallop, Polkinghorne and van Egmond.

The Matildas, the third youngest squad at the World Cup in Germany with thirteen debutants and an average age of 22, made the quarter-finals.

That's Sermanni's legacy. The group of 2023 was moulded in this era.

There were two wins in the group stage, following a tight 1-0 defeat by Brazil: 3-2 over Equatorial Guinea in Bochum and 2-1 against Norway in Leverkusen.

A young van Egmond's classy right-foot volley was the highlight in the first win. There were also goals from Leena Khamis and Lisa De Vanna, although the biggest story against Equatorial Guinea was a bizarre, comical handball incident, where one of their defenders caught the ball near the goal line, thinking they'd heard a whistle. Even after she caught it, and quickly let go, there was no whistle, and she got away with it! Weird.

Quality finishing from Kyah Simon helped her score a match-winning brace against a tricky Norway outfit, rewarding great service from De Vanna on the left, and then Kim Carroll from the right.

Once again, the Matildas found themselves with the world's elite in the knockout phase, and although Sweden ended our tournament, there was one almighty highlight.

Elysse Perry

Down 2-0, 21-year-old Ellyse Perry did something very, very special to get Australia back into the game.

The No. 6 wound up from beyond the edge of the area. Shooting from the right side of the field, she could not have struck the ball more perfectly with her left foot.

It was a sparkling goal from a player who lit the Australian sporting scene with her talent and personality.

Perry is one of the most incredible stories in Australian sport—the ultimate all-rounder who is the only player to play a cricket and football World Cup. A freakish talent, she made her international debut in both sports at 16, and among several records, she boasts the highest Test score by an Australian female cricketer (213 not out). Imagine scoring a goal like that at a football World Cup while casually bossing cricket at the highest level as well. Sports fans adored her, especially because she remained so humble throughout her success. Eventually, fixtures in both sports started to clash and by 2016, she was focused solely on cricket.

Her strike in 2011 was what we will remember, but a 3-1 defeat and exit was disappointing.

That tournament would prove so important for the future of the Tillies.

It was the first of four World Cups that teenage trio Kerr, Foord and van Egmond would play together, with Foord given the job of marking Brazil icon Marta in the opening game. A great responsibility; what an experience.

For van Egmond, it saw a proud Australian football name represented on the global stage, with dad Gary, an A-League Championship-winning coach and former Socceroo proudly watching on. His daughter went on to become one of the mainstays of the Tillies midfield ever since.

For Garriock, it was the end of her epic Matildas journey—one hundred and thirty games which started as a talented 16-year-old and spanned three World Cups, three Asian Cups and two Olympic Games while leading the charge also playing club football in America, Sweden, Denmark as well as at home.

Garriock retired at 29 at her peak. Hard-working, fit and with class in her left boot, she had so much more to give.

It might have been the end of an era on the park, but not the end of her changing the game off it.

At the time, it was impossible to be a mum and a travelling Matilda. So, Garriock continued to push for what was fair and right.

Today, when we see a Tillies squad, we're used to seeing kids giggling in dining halls or in videos on social media. Katrina Gorry's daughter Harper has even become a TikTok sensation.

It hasn't always been like that, and that's why today's stars always thank their pioneering heroes like Garriock. She made sure that football, such a part of her life from the moment she started playing with a team of boys at six years of age, would have a better future for females to aspire to be a part of.

Collette McCallum, Alicia Ferguson, Melissa Barbieri, Joanne Peters, Heather Garriock, Danielle Small, Cheryl Salisbury and Kathryn Gill at the 2011 World Cup, Hangzhou, China

50

It is not the most exciting part of the story, but it is almost the most important.

These talented athletes played for the love of the sport.

Now, the Matildas are one of the most recognisable teams in Australia. Just over ten years ago, that would have been hard to imagine.

Change was needed, especially as new names started popping up across the country getting minutes in Australia's W-League.

Perth had Sam Kerr; Elise Kellond-Knight, Tameka Yallop and Clare Polkinghorne were in Brisbane; there was Kyah Simon (Mariners), Emily van Egmond (Jets) and Lydia Williams (Canberra), followed by Steph Catley and Katrina Gorry (Victory), Hayley Raso (Canberra), Mackenzie Arnold (Perth), and Sydney-blooded Caitlin Foord and Alanna Kennedy.

Thanks to Garriock and her fellow pioneers, we are where we are now for the current generation and beyond. Equality, fairness and opportunity is important anywhere in society, and our football stars, the Matildas, were champions at making that possible in football.

We Won't Take a Backward Step: The Ange Postecoglou Era

2014 FIFA World Cup, Brazil

After South Africa, the sun started to set on our beloved Golden Generation—but cracks remained hidden for a while longer.

German Holger Osieck, who was assistant coach to football icon Franz Bekenbauer when West Germany won the 1990 FIFA World Cup, steered our veterans to the final of the 2011 Asian Cup, and in 2013, to the Brazil World Cup—our third straight qualification.

After three decades in exile, the green and gold were now World Cup regulars.

But that World Cup quest went down to the wire. In the final game of qualifying, we needed an 83rd-minute Josh Kennedy header, set up thanks to a perfect Mark Bresciano dink, to beat Iraq 1-0 in Sydney to seal our automatic spot. Giant striker Kennedy, known affectionately as Jesus because of his flowing long hair and matching beard, thankfully produced a miracle right when his country needed something special.

Fans wanted more. Despite the Asian Cup final, lost to Japan in extra-time, and qualifying for our third consecutive World Cup, Australia never fell in love with Osieck.

It ended in disaster.

Eight months from the Brazil World Cup, his side copped 12 goals in two friendlies in a humiliating month.

END OF AN ERA
September 8, 2013: Brazil 6, Australia 0
October 12, 2013: France 6, Australia 0

It was so harsh, even Brazil defender David Luiz, who played with Mark Schwarzer at Chelsea, said he felt sorry for his clubmate.

Brazil and France's sides were stacked. Our team looked finished.

"Most *embarrassing* pair of results in Socceroos history," screamed the *Sydney Morning Herald.*

Despite taking on names like Neymar (Barcelona), Thiago Silva (Paris Saint-Germain), David Luiz (Chelsea), Maicon (Roma), Marcelo (Real Madrid), Hugo Lloris (Tottenham), Raphael Varane (Real Madrid), Patrice Evra (Manchester United), Franck Ribery (Bayern Munich), Samir Nasri (Manchester City), Paul Pogba (Juventus) and Olivier Giroud (Arsenal), the results and performances were unforgivable. The Socceroos were in turmoil.

Football Australia CEO David Gallop flew to France and sacked Osieck then and there.

A World Cup was around the corner and the Socceroos badly needed a new inspiration.

Enter Ange Postecoglou.

Big Ange.

Long before the world knew him as a Premier League manager, Australian football was his backyard and field of dreams.

Since 2021, Ange Postecoglou has gone from arriving in Europe as Ange Postecogl-WHO to being known as one of the most attacking bosses in the *world.*

His teams play thrilling football to worldwide audiences. In Scotland, with Celtic, he won FIVE trophies from six available in two years with one of the sport's most famous clubs.

When he arrived in England to coach Tottenham Hotspur, it was as if he had appeared overnight.

Not at all. His journey is a lesson to anyone, doing anything, about perseverance. If you've got a dream and a belief, DO NOT ABANDON IT.

Did you know that in 2008 he could not even get a job at all in coaching? He was analysing games for *Fox Sports,* waiting for another chance. It was on TV we all got a little glimpse of what he would do if he took over a club, or even the Socceroos one day. Passion. Pride. Represent what it means to be Australian when you walk out in a gold jersey.

How did he end up without a job? After seven years coaching Australia's under-17s and under-20s, an argument in an infamous 2006 interview with Craig Foster on *SBS* left the talented coach on the outside. He coached Panachaiki in Greece's third division and even kept himself busy coaching kids' clinics in Melbourne when he came home.

He did not let go of his dreams. All he needed was a go.

Postecoglou's belief also hadn't left him.

After all, in the National Soccer League, Australia's former first division for club football, he won back-to-back championships in 1997 and 1998 at South Melbourne, where he is their favourite son. Ange was just 32 years of age when he won those titles, having retired early due to injury and a love of coaching. He was so young he was even coaching some of his old teammates.

Postecoglou made his own luck. He made it known he was ready for a shot. He put himself in the right place at the right time.

In 2009, A-League club Brisbane Roar urgently needed a new boss mid-season. Finally, Ange's phone rang. *You're hired.*

Postecoglou had not yet had a shot in the new competition, which started in 2005.

Until 2009, Sydney FC, Melbourne Victory, Adelaide United, Central Coast Mariners and Newcastle Jets had won all the silverware.

By the time Postecoglou left Queensland in 2012, he had changed the Roar, and the A-League, forever.

Twelve years later, fans still dream of the show he put on in Brisbane. It was so good that their nickname was *ROARCELONA.*

His side went thirty-six straight matches without losing—a record in all Australian sport; they won two championships and a premiership and he did it entirely his way, sacking players who didn't believe what he was doing, and bringing in players who could play his beautiful style of football.

German midfielder Thomas Broich, probably the best signing ever made in the A-League, says simply, "He was a visionary."

"He had no fear whatsoever," he told *Fox Sports*. "That's probably the one message that I want to try and get across to all the young players."

That bravery helped his side make football an art.

They were also winners who never gave up.

In 2011's Grand Final against Central Coast, Brisbane were losing 2-0 AFTER 117 MINUTES.

In the most incredible end to the season, Henrique and Erik Paartalu scored to make it 2-2 after 120 minutes, before the Roar stormed home to win on penalties against a baby-faced future Socceroos captain Maty Ryan. The opposition coach? Future Socceroos coach Graham Arnold.

We had the best view of a thrill that Europe is now getting a taste of twelve years later.

After backing it up the next season, he returned home to Melbourne to rebuild Victory, but just eighteen months later, his country came calling. They needed the best man for the job, and he was Australian.

What a comeback.

This was a man who, unfairly, was left on the scrapheap after dedicating part of his career to Australia's youth teams.

Now, he had a call from his country to make the Socceroos competitive in Brazil.

Days until the first World Cup game: two hundred and thirty-five. There wasn't much time, but he'd do it *his way*.

After Verbeek and Osieck, the Australian was a breath of fresh air.

He talked up Australian football.

He believed in it.

He wanted Australia to love the Socceroos.

Ange Postecoglou wanted the Socceroos to take on the world.

Squad checklist:
☑ Attacking football
☑ Belief

☑ Competitiveness
☑ Must be playing for their clubs
☑ Age is no barrier
☑ Do not disagree with this checklist

OUT

Lucas Neill (captain)

Mark Schwarzer

Brett Holman

David Carney

Sasa Ognenovski

Josh Kennedy

Archie Thompson

Luke Wilkshire

IN

Mat Ryan

Tom Rogic

Jason Davidson

Alex Wilkinson

Adam Taggart

Mat Leckie

Ivan Franjic

Ben Halloran

Massimo Luongo

Bailey Wright

In an ideal world, it would not have ended this way for so many of our legends, given all they had done for our sport and this team, but Postecoglou's plan meant it was time for urgent change.

No one can ever forget the role they played in getting our sport to where it is today.

In 2024, seven of the ten most-capped Socceroos still come from the 2006 and 2010 squads, such was the size of their contribution in our game.

1. Mark Schwarzer, 109
2. Tim Cahill, 108
3. Lucas Neill, 96
4. Brett Emerton, 95

Like for so many of us, Postecoglou's inspiration was his dad. He was driven by a desire to make him proud.

That's why he loved to attack; memories of years watching games together with the Greek community at South Melbourne, or discovering the delights of football from across the world however or wherever they could watch it on television, were filled with attacking, entertaining football.

Would Dad be entertained? Would he enjoy this performance?

That was how he judged himself.

So, he got down to work. It came with headlines. Lots of them.

Ange Postecoglou embraces talisman Tim Cahill

Legends of the game lost their spots.

Many thought the new coach was taking risks.

However, Brisbane fans knew exactly what he was doing because they had seen it before.

To the man himself, he had a plan. He needed to create a team to be proud of.

A team that was *fearless*. The same word Broich mentioned. To do that, he needed fresh legs, open minds and exciting talent to take on an intimidating World Cup group.

World No. 14 Chile

World No. 15 Netherlands

World No. 1 Spain

Fear?

No way.

Opportunity.

Bring it on.

Four years earlier, Australia started a World Cup game and focused on defending. Postecoglou brought a new mindset.

His son summed it up in a message to his dad at the World Cup draw: go and become a legend.

By the time the side lined up against Chile in Cuiaba, only six of the eleven from the Socceroos' last 6-0 loss against France were in the squad at all.

Mark Schwarzer and Brett Holman retired; Luke Wilkshire was left out of the final twenty-three-man squad when it was trimmed in Brazil and captain Lucas Neill wasn't even selected in the preliminary thirty-man squad.

Neill's end was sad. The Manly United junior had given so much to his country, was a great representative for the sport and reached incredible levels in the Premier League, with nearly ten years across Blackburn, West Ham and Everton. He did not want to leave the national team, but he had played just forty club games between 2011 and 2014.

By name, his was the toughest call. By form, Postecoglou had little choice but to give a chance to a younger player.

In this team, if you were good enough, you were old enough and it didn't matter which league you played in. No one owned the jersey; you earned the right to wear it.

Just ask A-League stars like Ivan Franjic, Matt McKay or Golden Boot winner Adam Taggart. Ask Massimo Luongo, plucked from England's lower leagues.

But no wins in 2014 against South Africa, Ecuador and Croatia had pundits asking questions about the squad's balance. Would it all come together in time?

Like he did at South Melbourne and Brisbane, and like he would do with Yokohama and Celtic, risk eventually equalled reward for Ange Postecoglou.

Looking at the cold facts now, the scoreboard doesn't flatter Australia in Brazil.

But it was a thrilling adventure, especially against Chile and the Netherlands. Australia was no disgrace in the world's eyes and it paved the way for silverware in 2015.

The opener, though, could have been a disaster. A young, nervous unit was 2-0 down after 14 minutes against Chile after a goal and assist from Barcelona star Alexis Sanchez, who moved to Arsenal after the World Cup.

The Socceroos, the lowest-ranked side in the tournament, could've crumbled.

Instead of hiding, they pushed harder.

Over the next 165 World Cup minutes against Chile and the Netherlands, they went toe-to-toe with football heavyweights, just like Postecoglou promised.

Cahill headed brilliantly off a Franjic cross to cool the nerves, and an equaliser looked likely until Jean Beausejour's 90th-minute goal to seal a 3-1 result for Chile.

Meanwhile our next opponent, the Netherlands, had put FIVE past Spain in a rematch of the 2010 World Cup final from four years prior.

Their lineup was ridiculous, headlined by:
- Inter Milan's Wesley Sneijder
- Manchester United's Robin van Persie
- Bayern Munich's Arjen Robben.

By contrast, Australia's highest-profile names were Cahill and Bresciano, but by 2014, the Everton icon was in America's Major League Soccer at the New York Red Bulls, and the former Serie A star from Italy's top division was now enjoying the slower pace in Qatar with Al-Gharafa.

Captain Mile Jedinak was a club hero at Premier League outfit Crystal Palace, while a group of youngsters like Mat Ryan, Jason Davidson, Mat Leckie, Tommy Oar, James Holland, Mitch Langerak and Dario Vidosic were breaking into Europe in Holland, Belgium, Austria, Germany and Switzerland.

What we had, though, was a *team*. Australians who would run through brick walls for Postecoglou, their mates and their country.

**Tim Cahill unleashes for
one of the goals of the tournament**
at the 2014 World Cup vs Netherlands

But against such amazing squads with so little time to prepare, why did the new coach make such radical changes when he had those older players who knew the big stage inside out?

This was a new era, and Ange had his eyes on the Asian Cup to be hosted by Australia in 2015.

The last thing he wanted was players not ready for that Asian Cup stage, especially if some Socceroos retired after the tournament in Brazil. He needed to form a group perfectly balanced between youth and experience who would be peaking on home soil in 2015. A team who could transform the Socceroos like Brisbane transformed the A-League.

Some might say that June 19, 2014, Australia's pulsating 3-2 defeat to the Netherlands, who finished third at the World Cup, was the day it all started to make sense to those who doubted the plan. "Postecoglou promised his players would take the game to Holland," crowed *The Guardian.* "The coach was true to his word."

The Socceroos almost—and should've—caused a boil-over. What a game.

Arjen Robben opened the scoring 20 minutes in.

From the kick-off, right-back Ryan McGowan floated a cross from deep on the right side of the field to the far post on the left. Immediately after conceding a goal, this side was looking forward. Quickly.

There have been some iconic, defining moments in Australian sport. But very few have left the watching world gasping, jaws dropped, like what happened next.

Cahill watched the ball sail towards him.

Eyes on the ball.

Dreaming of the impossible.

Then, thump. The *sweetest, purest* **thump**.

It was the most astonishing strike an Australian had unleashed on the world stage.

Shock.

Joy.

Pride.

World-class.

GAME ON.

1-1.

Cahill ran to the corner flag to unleash his trademark flurry of punches at a THIRD World Cup.

Everything else about this goal was not typical, though.

Cahill, a player known for his attitude, work ethic and incredible ability to score with his head, produced a **LEFT-FOOT VOLLEY** with such a high degree of difficulty that it was compared to Dutch legend Marco van Basten's Euro 1988 final volley. That goal is called one of the greatest ever scored (check it out on YouTube). That's one heck of a comparison.

Once again, Cahill was defying the odds, like he had done his whole career.

TIM CAHILL
108 Socceroos games
50 Socceroos goals

AUSTRALIA'S WORLD CUP GOAL SCORERS
Five: Tim Cahill
Three: Mile Jedinak
Two: Brett Holman
One: Craig Goodwin, Mitch Duke, Mathew Leckie, Harry Kewell,
Craig Moore, John Aloisi, own goal

If you ever feel like your football is not going to plan, just remember this: Australia's greatest male goal scorer of all time did not play once for a junior national Australian side.

In fact, we nearly lost him.

He played for a Western Samoa under-20s side. It almost made him unable to ever represent Australia. Thankfully, after a lot of work behind the scenes from then coach Frank Farina, he could.

Cahill forced his way to the top with his incredible, determined focus, starring for Millwall in England's second division (the Championship) as they miraculously made the 2004 FA Cup final. Always a man for the biggest stage, he scored the winning goal in the semi-final too.

At Everton, he is quite simply, an icon.

He was known for his incredible heading ability and admired for his goals, all 56 of them. But none were quite like this one.

Colombia's James Rodriguez won the FIFA Goal of the Tournament at the 2014 World Cup, but many thought Cahill's classic left-foot volley against the Netherlands was the worthy winner. It still regularly gets replayed on FIFA's social channels.

"You dream as a kid for these opportunities," Cahill beamed.

"At home, in my garden, I score that every day … but this is what it's all about."

Australia enjoyed a storming start to the second-half, and when Oliver Bozanic's cross struck Daryl Janmaat's hand in the box, Jedinak stepped up from the penalty spot to put the Socceroos ahead.

Oh. My. Goodness. AUSTRALIA LEAD.

Sadly, the high lasted four minutes, as Premier League legend van Persie smashed an equaliser, but Australia had an INCREDIBLE chance to score a third when McKay pinched the ball and sparked an attack. Oar crossed for Leckie, open at the back post, but had he shot or passed more deftly, who knows what might have been.

The Dutch oozed quality. Sub Memphis Depay—you might know him from his Manchester United, Barcelona or Atletico Madrid fame—fizzed the winner past Ryan.

WHAT A GAME
20' Robben goal: 0-1
21' Cahill goal: 1-1
54' Jedinak goal: 2-1
58' van Persie goal: 2-2
68' Depay goal: 2-3

What a game of football; one of the few moments where the world was talking about us. Holland's Louis van Gaal, one of football's most famous bosses, was so wound up by the game he refused to shake Postecoglou's hand! "I liked that, it told me we were on the right path," Postecoglou wrote in his book, *Changing the Game*.

However, the loss meant Australia was eliminated. In a 'dead rubber' game against Spain, with Cahill suspended, La Rojas cruised to a 3-0 triumph. The goal scorers? Fernando Torres, David Villa and Juan Mata.

What an experience for the young Australians.

Adam Taggart against Sergio Ramos.

Matt McKay, Mile Jedinak and Olivier Bozanic v Xabi Alonso, Andres Iniesta and Koke.

Mathew Leckie v Jordi Alba.

Come January 2015, football fans in Australia would celebrate the benefits.

THE 2015 ASIAN CUP

Melbourne: Australia 4, Kuwait 1

Brisbane: Australia 0, South Korea 1

Sydney: Australia 4, Oman 0

Brisbane: Australia 2, China 0

Newcastle: Australia 2, United Arab Emirates 0

Sydney: Australia 2, South Korea 1 (after extra-time)

To those old enough to remember the 2015 Asian Cup hosted by Australia, it was a simply joyous and surprising month, on and off the park.

First, Australia won its first senior male international trophy.

The nation also came out with beautiful and colourful crowds. Four group stage matches were sold out, including Japan v Jordan in Melbourne and China v DPR Korea in Canberra. Our communities embraced the Asian Cup and showed the different parts of our society. To those who thought no one would care about the tournament, Australia's football-loving public stood up and also showed the best of multicultural Australia.

With such fond memories, it's easy to forget how much work had to be done.

Australia only won one friendly out of five after the 2014 World Cup, and was even defeated by South Korea in the group stage of the Asian Cup, leaving the Socceroos in second place in Group A.

It was a Socceroos lineup without any superstars, but it had twenty-three Australian footballers who were young, fearless and talented.

Maty Ryan, 22, was a future captain.

Trent Sainsbury, 23, another Central Coast graduate, was the heart of the defence.

It was a great time to be a young attacking player.

Mat Leckie, 23, and Robbie Kruse, 26, had the starting spots flanking Tim Cahill, 35, but opportunities were there for Tommy Oar, 23, Nathan Burns, 26, Terry Antonis, 21, James Troisi, 26, and Tomi Juric, 23.

Players who are now Australian football royalty—Mile Jedinak, 30, Mark Milligan, 29, and Mark Bresciano, 34—provided a perfect balance.

A decade after Bresciano scored *that* goal against Uruguay, he still remained

Captain **Mile Jedinak** with the Asian Cup

a rare gem in Australian football: a gifted, silky, creative midfielder whose Socceroos highlights reel is just a showcase of the kind of quality everyone wants to watch. It is why Postecoglou made sure he was still involved in 2015, despite being in his twilight years, playing club football in the Middle East.

His is one of the most accomplished careers we've watched, competing in Italy's Serie A from 1999 to 2011 with Empoli, Parma, Palermo and Lazio. Early on, he had his mate Vince Grella alongside him. Bresciano and Grella, the tough-tackling defensive midfielder, great character and the Socceroos' resident parmesan cheese supplier, also played together for Carlton in Victoria and enhanced Australia's reputation in Italy. They were quite the duo— and their partnership remains intact today in business, where they run Italian club Catania amongst other interests.

Just how good was he? Grella told *Optus Sport* in 2021 that his mate, signed by Parma for a then Australian record of $11 million, could have played for Italy. "He would have played for the Italian national team, 100 per cent," he said. Lucky for us, he was a Socceroo. Uruguay 2005. The crosses for Kewell in 2006 and Kennedy in 2013. The list goes on. It simply wouldn't be the same story without him.

But *the story* of this tournament would become Massimo Luongo.

WHO?!

The shy, unknown midfielder plucked from the third division of English football who became the player of the tournament.

If you're good enough, you're old enough, wherever you play.

Attention to detail is everything to get to the top, and Postecoglou scouted everyone, everywhere.

At the 2015 Asian Cup, Luongo was a lesson to all of us in believing in your ability even when others question why you are there. His boss believed in him; that's what mattered.

The 22-year-old was spectacular.

He was so good, he was nominated for the 2015 Ballon d'Or, the world footballer of the year award, despite playing for League One club Swindon Town. Who won it that year? Some guy called … Lionel Messi.

Persistence continued to be a theme for Luongo throughout his career. In August 2024, thirteen years after arriving in England to join Tottenham's youth set-up, he finally made his Premier League debut. He was a key part of Ipswich's epic journey from League One to the Championship to the Premier League in back-to-back seasons, and started for them against Liverpool at 31 years of age as the club celebrated its first season in the top division in twenty-two years. "It's massive," he told *Optus Sport*. "(On a) personal note, it's incredible for my background, for my story … it feels good."

The Asian Cup started comfortably enough for the Socceroos against Kuwait and Oman. After concern over where Australia's goals would come from if not from Cahill, the hosts had eight goal scorers in two outings: Cahill, Luongo, Jedinak, Troisi, McKay, Kruse, Milligan and Juric.

A 1-0 loss to South Korea was a curveball but Australia was too strong for China, and then got a massive favour from the United Arab Emirates, who knocked Japan out in a quarter-final shootout.

Cahill was the man again in Brisbane. He had his Weet-Bix and scored from a breathtaking bicycle kick as well as a classic header from Davidson's cross.

In Newcastle, Sainsbury rose to head Luongo's third-minute corner home, before Davidson bundled home a 14th-minute goal. The hosts were now in the swing of the tournament with three clean sheets and ten scorers. South Korea beat 2007 champions Iraq to set up the final.

Long before Postecoglou made Son Heung-Min his Tottenham captain, he knew the talent of his South Korean ace because he almost ruined Australia's 2015 Asian Cup final party.

Ninety-one minutes into a gripping final, another famous night at Stadium Australia, Son, then at German club Bayer Leverkusen, levelled at 1-1.

Gasps. Silence. What!

How could this be?

This was supposed to be the night that Postecoglou's plan all came together. Do we do anything easily in Australian football?

NOPE.

The hosts had led in Sydney since Luongo's simply sublime 45th-minute strike, his crowning moment in the tournament.

It is one of the great goals scored by an Australian.

If there is a moment that represents Postecoglou's side's best qualities, this could be it: central defender Sainsbury drove bravely into midfield and pierced a pass forward and quickly into Luongo's path.

Luongo's positioning, turn, and deft touch were masterful. The poise, confidence and style in the strike completed his masterpiece.

But with the celebrations about to begin, the Socceroos were stunned by Son Heung-Min and needed to refocus.

As South Korea's players slumped, tired before extra-time, Postecoglou spotted them trying to find the energy for another 30 minutes. He seized the moment.

A coaching masterclass.

"Look at them," he said to his team in a huddle.

The coach reminded his players how fit they were. **They were made for this moment.** He asked them to be the heroes.

"This," he said in a brilliant, quick speech. "This will make it even better!"

Step up, Tomi Juric. Step up, James Troisi.

Juric charged down the right of the box, refusing to give up. He wanted it MORE. He kept going. Hassled. He won the ball and set up Troisi.

PARTY TIME.

Troisi surged to the sideline to celebrate with 76,000 fans.

It was a moment of beauty: the first time that the Socceroos had won a major senior international trophy.

In Oceania, Australia won tournaments all the time. But this was different.

Jedinak lifted the trophy high into the Sydney sky.

And as he had done everywhere, Ange Postecoglou delivered the promise of silverware so many had doubted and he did it his way. The nation was in love with the Socceroos again.

Introducing the World Number Four!

2015 FIFA Women's World Cup, Canada

Getting to Canada presented some hurdles for the Matildas.

The team didn't make the 2012 Olympics, and Dutch coach Hesterine de Reus' stint ended quickly.

Her exit opened the door for popular Sydney FC boss Alen Stajcic, who immediately guided the Matildas to the 2014 Asian Cup final, losing 1-0 to Japan in Vietnam.

A talented group now had a leader in charge who arrived with two W-League premierships and two championships under his belt. He wanted his national team to showcase the best of our country.

STAJ CHECKLIST

- ☑ Positivity
- ☑ Back yourself
- ☑ Take it to the opponent
- ☑ Believe you can beat anyone

They needed all of that, too, with a 2015 World Cup group that would test their progress.

GROUP D, 'GROUP OF DEATH'

USA: World No. 2

Nigeria: Africa Champions
Sweden: World No. 5
Round of 16, Brazil: World No. 3

Ultimately, the Matildas proved they were a force in the women's game, making it through to the final eight.

Elise Kellond-Knight also achieved something no other Aussie has done. She was named in both the 2011 and 2015 World Cup Team of the Tournament, but as a defender in 2011 and a midfielder in 2015! KK missed the 2023 World Cup through injury but we got to enjoy the thoughts of one of the country's most intelligent players as she became a TV star.

MATILDAS LEAD THE WAY

1. *First senior side to win a trophy in Asia (2010)*
2. *First senior team to win a World Cup knockout game (2015)*
3. *First senior team to make a World Cup semi-final (2023)*
4. *Elise Kellond-Knight twice named in the World Cup Team of the Tournament (2011, 2015)*

MATILDAS ON THE RISE: FIFA WORLD RANKINGS

2003: 16
2004: 15
2005: 15
2006: 15
2007: 12
2008: 14
2009: 14
2010: 12
2011: 10
2012: 9
2013: 9
2014: 10
2015: 10

The Matildas opened by giving tournament heavyweights USA a mighty scare, but goals to rock stars Megan Rapinoe (two) and Christen Press sealed a 3-1 win. The US tried to unsettle Stajcic's Aussies with a tough game plan. But there were great signs from Australia's attack, forcing star goalie Hope Solo into a number of saves.

Emily van Egmond impressed, as did Gorry and Kellond-Knight.

Lisa De Vanna levelled the match at 1-1, deservedly, with a low, hard finish.

The fiery, brilliantly talented De Vanna is one of the most exciting attacking weapons our country has ever produced. In Canada, she scored her SEVENTH World Cup goal spanning three tournaments.

Explosive. Unpredictable. Competitive. De Vanna was a thrill to watch— and she played her way.

DE VANNA BY THE NUMBERS
Games: 150
Goals: 47
World Cups: 4
Olympics: 2
W-League Championships: 5

She had a fearless approach, which grew, like so many of her era, from playing with her brothers and neighbours in Fremantle, Western Australia. Nothing scared her, and why should it, with her dribbling skills.

There was so much Aussie spirit in the combative De Vanna and a love of football running deeply through her Portuguese and Italian roots. De Vanna had a fearless streak because like so many of our greats, she had to take risks.

She left Perth at 16 and had to push past her reputation as a rebel.

Yet here she was, leading her country out at a World Cup.

"All I ever wanted to do is something great," she said. "Big, be a part of history."

Rather than being disappointed after game one against the US, the Matildas felt their hard work would pay off, taking positives from a match they dominated for long periods.

Lisa De Vanna

Against Nigeria, Kyah Simon's brace got their tournament up and running. Her goals were set up by another dazzling De Vanna run, and a Kerr cross.

The side then qualified for the knockout phase after a tense 1-1 draw with Sweden. The game-breaker?

De Vanna, of course.

She opened the scoring, striding towards goal thanks to Laura Alleway's pass five minutes in, but Sweden hit back ten minutes later. The game swung back and forth, with Lydia Williams performing heroics in goal. The win meant the Aussies got revenge for their 2011 exit at Sweden's hands, while progressing

73

to the next stage was an almighty success for this young group of stars.

Suddenly, the Matildas were getting some more attention. We know today how much interest there is in female sport, but in 2015, it was only just about to erupt. Our Matildas were at the front of that wave.

Next up, Brazil. Almighty Brazil, a familiar foe who were becoming quite the rival.

When you think about football royalty, male or female, the famous yellow jersey—a strip that never changes—comes to mind.

But in the elite women's football space, Australia was entering that top tier of nations. This proved it.

HISTORY-MAKERS: THE FIRST AUSSIE XI TO WIN A KNOCKOUT GAME
Williams; Foord, Alleway, Kennedy, Catley; Kellond-Knight, van Egmond, Butt; De Vanna, Heyman, Kerr

Locked at 0-0, Stajcic brought Katrina Gorry and Kyah Simon off the bench. It proved to be a masterstroke.

With ten minutes left, Simon was quickest to pounce after the Brazilian goalkeeper spilled De Vanna's strike.

Gorry started the move, linking with De Vanna. Simon finished it. Super subs.

1-0 to the Matildas.

Simon sprinted off, two fists pumping, mobbed by teammates. This was big.

Stajcic called it his greatest moment in football.

Foord, like in 2011, silenced Marta, the *Pele of women's football*.

Williams kept another clean sheet.

Kellond-Knight summed it up: *"super proud"*.

How good of a win was it? Brazil simply couldn't believe it. It was the only goal they conceded in Canada. Now, they were out.

"Yes!!! I love this team," Simon wrote on Twitter.

"Doubt or belief in us, we don't care, it drives us!"

For Simon, who would miss 2019 with injury, and then make the 2023 squad but get injured, this was one of her great moments.

STORIES FROM THE BIGGEST STAGE ON EARTH

It isn't just the players who give so much to get to these moments. Someone must take you to training when you're a kid, and so many families sacrificed so much for these moments.

Simon, one of Australia's most successful Indigenous athletes—the first male or female indigenous footballer to score at a World Cup—says of her mum and dad, "Everything I achieved in my career is because of them."

And in the stands that day against Brazil sat her mum, dad and brother. It was too expensive to fly, so they drove. They drove for *two and a half days* **each way** to make sure they were there.

The sacrifice was worth it.

Simon was Stajcic's match-winner in Moncton, the crowning moment in a career dedicated to growing the profile of women's football.

Like Postecoglou who was delivering similar messages at the same time, Stajcic was heavily inspired by his dad's love of football that he brought with him from Yugoslavia in Europe. Like Ange, he also moved quickly into coaching. By 2015, he had devoted fifteen years to the cause.

He was a **believer**, long before it became popular to believe in women's football.

"We want people to see what a great sport this is," he said in a 2015 interview with *The Guardian*.

"Imagine hosting here in 2023, and a successful Matildas team. The sport would go through the roof."

That is what we call a prophecy coming true!

His side, still with an average age of just 23, were three minutes from taking World and Asian champions Japan to extra-time in their next game in Edmonton.

Mana Iwabuchi's winning goal sent the Matildas home, but this was a breakthrough tournament.

Alen Stajcic

This was now a team that *believed* on the world stage.

Fast. Skilful. Powerful. Brave.

"We don't want to compete with the best," Stajcic concluded. "We want to be the best."

That included work off the park where today's heroes stood up for what they believed in.

They were *elite* on the park, despite conditions not making it easy for them, or being rewarded for their achievements. So, they did not just want to stand up for their own rights or for more money. They wanted to improve the future, to make it possible for young girls to make a career in football, something any girl could—or should—want to chase.

That's a legacy to leave.

You can now dream big, and that's no small thanks to these players who had an idea and fought for it.

Just months after Canada, the highs of Brazil and with the rare focus of the Australian sporting public on them, the Matildas boycotted a glamorous set of games against the USA to continue to fight for the rights of female footballers.

They were serious. And they got their point across.

Lydia Williams, reflecting on that big moment, told *Fox Sports*, "That was … pretty monumental in the women's game."

A deal was eventually struck for improving working conditions for Matildas' players, and they continued to get fine-tuned over the coming years.

For everything they achieved on the park, fighting for equality is something to be equally proud of.

Williams was at the forefront of that campaign. The goalkeeper from Kalgoorlie, Western Australia, went on to become Australia's longest-serving Matilda. What a contribution on and off the park.

"I started in this team as a teenager from Canberra and across almost two decades I never imagined that I would be afforded the opportunity to learn, grow, experience life's challenges and joys, fight against injustices and be shaped into the person I am today," she said when announcing her Matildas retirement.

It is one of the more remarkable careers, given as a kid it was an AFL ball that she would kick barefoot in the bush. At 11, when her family moved to Canberra, she was thrown in goals because there were no other spots left. When she saved a penalty in her first game, there was no looking back.

Lyds retired in 2024 after twenty years of national service: five World Cups, six Asian Cups and three Olympic Games. Her father, who encouraged her love of sport, passed away the year before her Matildas debut—but Williams honours his legacy with her achievements, which includes an outstanding club career in Australia and abroad, including stints at clubs like Manchester City and Paris Saint-Germain. The beautiful children's books she has penned shares her pride in her Indigenous culture and her unique football journey with an entirely new generation.

On the park, Stajcic's side continued to rise:

- ☑ Qualifying for their first Olympics in twelve years in 2016
- ☑ Agonisingly close to knocking Brazil out of their own Rio Olympics in 2016, edged 7-6 in a quarter-final penalty shootout
- ☑ Winning the Tournament of Nations against the USA, Japan and Brazil in 2017—their first trophy in seven years, beating Brazil 6-1 as De Vanna, Foord, Kerr and Gorry ran riot
- ☑ A first ever win over the USA in 2017
- ☑ World ranking in December 2017: FOUR

This period saw the Sam Kerr story really start to take off, becoming a juggernaut.

The W-League star scored a hat-trick against Japan in the Tournament of Nations, was scoring for fun in the local league and had kids falling in love with her incredible backflips. She played with a freedom and smile that made you feel like she was your mate next door.

By the time Brazil arrived for a friendly series in September 2017, she was the main act—and delivered—with goals in the 2-1 and 3-2 wins to notch seven in her last four games.

Think back to 2007 and 2011 when Brazil were the big guns. Now, the Matildas had three straight triumphs over them, as they hit a record five-game winning streak overall.

It might seem odd to be writing about friendlies in this story of World Cups, but these games signalled that something special was simmering.

Fifteen thousand fans watched in Penrith.

Sixteen thousand in Newcastle.

Many of these sold-out games were played during AFL and NRL finals, yet the Matildas had the media and public's attention.

Stajcic first noticed it back in 2017. The Matildas hype didn't start in 2023. It started to snowball earlier as stadiums increasingly became a sea of gold with families, young girls and boys, mums and dads, all happily cheering with banners and signs everywhere.

"This was the week football really turned in Australia," Stajcic beamed in 2017 as his side, who used to play in front of family, friends and not much more, became one of the hottest tickets in town.

THE PROGRESS
2006, Asian Cup final crowd, Adelaide: 5,000
2015 World Cup farewell game crowd, Sydney: 4,277
Streaks of sold-out home games in May 2024: 13

Heading into an Asian Cup and World Cup cycle, a new crop of exciting stars were emerging as well.

The remarkable teenage fullback Ellie Carpenter, midfielder Chloe Logarzo, attacker Hayley Raso and goalkeeper Mackenzie Arnold were some of the now familiar names breaking into the side's core group.

Everything was looking good.

Or so it seemed.

No Movie is as Unpredictable as Football

2018 FIFA World Cup, Russia

After 2005, Australian sports fans got comfortable making World Cups. Life was good.

The Socceroos were Asian champions, but that made them the hunted.

Everyone wanted to knock over Ange's side—and the road to the World Cup in Russia was the nation's biggest test yet in Asia.

Football is constantly improving across Asia, especially in areas where huge amounts of money are being pumped into the sport. It is not so in Australia. Amongst many reasons, the simplest is that we play so many sports, while across the planet, football is often at the heart of society.

Postecoglou wanted to dominate the region by playing aggressive football.

One of the many challenges of playing in Asia is the sheer size of the continent; it is a planning nightmare trying to get the team from game to game—even for home fixtures, with players arriving from all over the planet to get to our great, but far away, southern land.

It is a challenge few nations experience. Ahead of most games, the coach is lucky to get three training sessions with his side, and each away game presents different hurdles. The 2010 squad was ruthless in this mission; the 2014 group squeezed through in the final game. The 2018 group went on a roller coaster ride.

The longest qualifying journey of any nation in World Cup history

- 22 games
- 37 players
- 11 countries
- $10 million spent
- 250,000 kilometres travelled
- 29 months

Learning geography through the world game: Australia's away trips

Middle East: Jeddah, Saudi Arabia. Amman, Jordan. Abu Dhabi, UAE.

Central Asia: Bishkek, Kyrgyzstan. Dushanbe, Tajikistan.

East Asia: Saitama, Japan.

South Asia: Dhaka, Bangladesh.

Southeast Asia: Bangkok, Thailand.

Relocated due to conflict: Iraq played in Tehran, Iran. Syria played in Malacca, Malaysia.

Central America: San Pedro Sula, Honduras.

START: JUNE 17, 2015
END: NOVEMBER 15, 2017

As late as October 2016, it looked as though it would be business as usual in terms of the Socceroos' World Cup qualification. But in November, the heat turned up. Group minnows Thailand held the Aussies to a 2-2 draw in sapping weather in Bangkok.

Premier League watchers, especially Spurs fans, will know all about Postecoglou's commitment to his belief in building to something bigger. He won't change, no matter how many ways the media asks him to. How do you build something if you change as soon as it doesn't work? He wanted to create an Australian way of playing to be proud of and to take on the world. To do that, he wanted to play a formation with three central defenders, making more attacking options available up the field.

As cracks in qualifying started to appear, criticism became fierce: was the national team boss choosing the wrong time to experiment, risking a World Cup spot?

What would you do? Stick with what you believe in or change?

Do you truly know what you believe in? If you do, it can help guide you when times get tough.

For Ange Postecoglou, he didn't just want to stumble into a World Cup. He wanted to take a team that knew what it believed in and what it stood for; a team that could show off the best of Australia to the biggest audience on the planet.

The maths was getting tighter on the table, however, even after Australia took six points against UAE and Saudi Arabia, thanks to a glorious Tom Rogic long-range goal in Adelaide against the Saudis.

Before the climax of qualifying, Australia was invited as Asian champions to the 2017 Confederations Cup, a World Cup test event in Russia. They were breathtaking at times, providing a glimpse into what the coach was trying to build. Australia were edged 3-2 by Germany before 1-1 draws with Cameroon, the champions of Africa, and Chile, South America's Copa America winners.

But when World Cup qualifying kicked off again in August 2017, it was three months of chaos.

1. **August 31:** 2-0 loss in Japan.
2. **September 5:** Beat Thailand 2-1 in Melbourne but Saudi Arabia and Japan finish ahead on the table, taking the automatic World Cup spots. Australia would have to go to the play-offs.
3. **October 5:** Face war-torn Syria in Malaysia. 1-1.
4. **October 10:** Tim Cahill's 109TH-MINUTE extra-time winner seals a nervous win against Syria over two legs. Syria hit the post with the last kick of the game; had it gone in, Australia would have been out on the 'away goals' rule.
5. **October 11:** *The Herald Sun* newspaper drops a bombshell report saying Ange Postecoglou will QUIT the national team EVEN IF Australia qualifies. It kicked off a month of hysteria around the side. Is it true? Will he or won't he? Why is he?
6. **November 11:** The Socceroos play out a tense 0-0 draw in Central America against Honduras. San Pedro Sula, at the time, was one of the most dangerous crime cities in the world.

7. **November 15:** A Mile Jedinak hat-trick in Sydney ends the World Cup marathon. A fourth straight World Cup, you beauty!

8. **November 21:** Ange Postecoglou resigns.

Unlike previous campaigns, there was a feeling of relief, not ecstasy at the end.

Everyone was exhausted: players, the media and fans. None more so than Ange Postecoglou.

He wanted to transform Australian football as the national team leader—take it to a promised land. After the long, winding road to Russia, though, he decided not to continue. There were too many hurdles. He had such big dreams for Australian football, his exit left many confused, and plenty sad. They wanted to see the end of the journey at the World Cup, together. But he had his reasons and his own dreams and didn't want to be held back.

Australia celebrate defeating Honduras to qualify for Russia 2018 with three goals from captain Mile Jedinak

Now in his fifties, he is well and truly living those dreams in the centre of the football universe.

His time in charge takes up a big chunk of this story. Yes, because he won the nation's only senior male trophy, but also because his journey, and his leadership, are loaded with so many lessons.

He wanted to make his dad proud. He overcame incredible professional obstacles to reach the top. He never lost his ambition nor his commitment to what he believed in. It is hard not to admire his passion, focus and dedication.

An Aussie, who was coaching kids in a park in 2008, became the boss of a Premier League powerhouse, and is loved in Japan and Scotland.

We Aussies might be a blip on the other side of the football world, but we can keep reaching new milestones with dreams, talent and incredible hard work. Ange has proven that for all of us.

So did our first wave of pioneers, like **Joe Marston**, the first Aussie to play in an FA Cup final for Preston North End in 1954; **Craig Johnston**, who was a Liverpool rock star in the 1980s, and our two Premier League winners, **Robbie Slater** (Blackburn 1995) and **Mark Bosnich** (Manchester United 2000). They put Australia on the map, opening doors for players; now Postecoglou

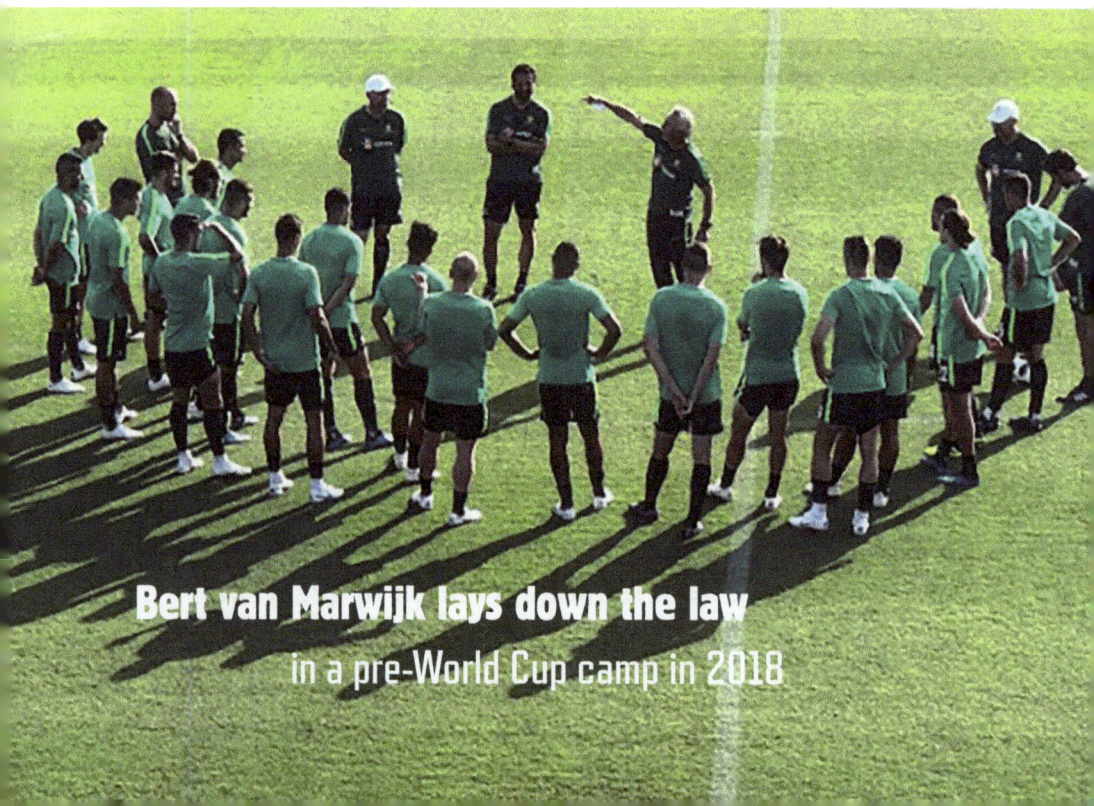

Bert van Marwijk lays down the law in a pre-World Cup camp in 2018

is doing the same for coaches.

He might not have finished how he had dreamed of as the Australian coach. But he has continued to shape the game for our country since making his big decision. His extraordinary results have reminded the world that there is great talent and knowledge here in Australian football.

Football, you'll learn, is a funny old game. That is what makes it so addictive.

You'll love it. But just like family, you'll get mad at it. It hurts you, sometimes betrays you. Shocks you! Then, you forgive it, and do it all again.

It is the most wonderful hobby, an escape from everyday life that becomes an essential part of it.

The highs are moments in time you cherish.

The lows are lessons you learn from in your everyday life. How do you react when you lose, when you're benched or when you're injured?

It can form bonds and create friendships. It provides a reason for connection that might not be there otherwise.

It is a sport, but so much more.

Playing it keeps you healthy. It makes you social.

Football pushes and tests you.

How many of you support your team because your dad or mum do? And they supported that team because one of your grandparents did?

It is like a tradition. It makes you closer to those you share it with.

Religion is handed down from generation to generation. So, too, is football. No wonder it is often called a religion!

So often, football is the one religion that solves conflicts. It is the one topic that crosses over different languages when it should be a barrier.

The game has highlights that are now like a digital treasure box.

Its history is mesmerising.

Our history reads like a drama.

What makes it even better than a movie?

NO ONE knows what is about to happen next…

There is enough drama in football—and that's before you add the word "Australia" to it. Then you've got something even more unpredictable, and 2016-2018 was one heck of a roller coaster.

Once again, Australia was staring down a World Cup without a coach in charge.

In came a 65-year-old Dutch veteran, Bert van Marwijk, who coached *against* Australia during qualifying. He left Saudi Arabia after a disagreement and was looking for a World Cup ticket. Good timing for everyone.

Like Verbeek and Osieck, he was not a daring coach.

In other words, he was the *anti*-Ange.

Bert van Marwijk was no mug, though. He was the Netherlands' coach when they made the 2010 World Cup final. That side was tough and rough. Have you ever seen Nigel de Jong's studs-up tackle in the final they lost to Spain? It summed up an approach that left many happy the artistic Spanish beat a nasty Netherlands.

There is no right or wrong way to play. Variety is one of the beauties of football; like life, it presents you with choices. Do you play for the adventure or the thrill of winning? Or do you play not to lose? Can you find a balance between those?

In a camp before the World Cup, the new boss gathered his team in a huddle and told them about the virtues of Atletico Madrid.

Have you ever watched them in La Liga or the Champions League? They're a brilliantly competitive side but they defend for their lives. They scrap, torment, retreat, niggle and then play a bit.

Australians had to get used to change, quickly. Ange-Ball was now history.

Australia was well prepared and competitive in Russia—and there was no better test than against eventual champions France to open the tournament. It was 0-0 at the break in the first game.

The Socceroos then became the answer to a trivia question when Josh Risdon's foul on Antoine Griezmann became the first World Cup penalty awarded by the VAR, which he converted.

Mark Milligan

Impressively, the underdogs hit back just four minutes later via a Jedinak penalty following a handball in the box.

A point, maybe, against one of the sport's powerhouses?

France's lineup on paper was one of the best ever assembled: Hugo Lloris, Raphael Varane, N'Golo Kante, Kylian Mbappe, Olivier Giroud, Ousmane Dembele, Antoine Griezmann, to name a few.

With ten minutes to go, Pogba wound up from distance and a deflection off Aziz Behich handed them the win.

Australia impressed, with France's boss Didier Deschamps, who also captained his country to a World Cup trophy in 1998, admitting, "It was a difficult game."

Bert van Marwijk settled on a group of players he trusted. Andrew Nabbout was the bolt from the blue, charging into the squad after unstoppable A-League form with the Newcastle Jets. Proof, again, that good form is hard to ignore.

The player *everyone* wanted to talk about, though, was teenager Daniel Arzani. Nineteen years old, he was the youngest player in the entire World Cup, and Australia's youngest ever, rewarded for a few dazzling Melbourne City performances that showed he was a proper talent. Arzani sparkled in Russia but his career has been a warning: for all the talent he showed, he has only just returned to the national team six years after bursting onto the scene. It is a credit to him that he has, after his progress stalled due to injury, some poor club moves, and perhaps enjoying too much hype too quickly.

BERT VAN MARWIJK'S AUSTRALIA

Ryan

Risdon   Sainsbury   Milligan   Behich

Kruse   Mooy   Jedinak (c)   Leckie

Rogic

Nabbout

At the other end of the age scale, Cahill was chasing history—a goal at a fourth-straight World Cup.

While he was pivotal for Ange in qualifying, van Marwijk only used him sparingly, despite the public begging for him to be more involved.

The Socceroos' dreams hung on games against Denmark and Peru in Samara and Sochi.

Against the Danes, Christian Eriksen, then at Tottenham, smacked a shot past Ryan, before a Leckie header was handballed in the box. Penalty.

Jedinak stepped up—again. He'd never missed a penalty for his country; the sixth man to score for his nation at a World Cup brought up his third goal in the competition.

The *Beard to Be Feared* retired from the national team after the tournament and goes down as one of our all-time greats. It is amazing that he captained his country in two World Cups, because he had to fight so hard to have a professional football career at all.

He was actually overlooked when the A-League started but was subsequently picked up by the Central Coast Mariners and did not look back, forcing his way into the Socceroos while earning a life-changing move to Turkey, where he caught the attention of English Championship club Crystal Palace. A determined, combative midfielder, Jedinak's smarts and skills were underrated, because his intimidating beard made him better-known for being such a tough player in the middle of the park.

He was a top-class leader, adored not just by his country, but by every club he played for. He was Palace's captain when they were promoted to the Premier League, where he became known as one of the most solid midfielders in a division full of midfield stars.

That's an amazing 'what if'. Imagine if Jedinak gave up after his initial rejection. Instead, he knuckled down with Sydney United and used adversity as a chapter in his football journey, not an end point.

Respect.

That's what Jedinak attracts from teammates everywhere. No wonder Aston Villa, his final club, kept him on as a scout and coach before Postecoglou called for his old skipper to join his coaching team at Spurs.

Jedinak was Ange's man. You could argue his greatest moment in green and gold came in Postecoglou's last game against Honduras. Not only did he score a hat-trick from penalties and free-kicks, but he completed 180 minutes within four days—which was more than he had played all season due to injury.

A 'JEDI MASTER'

Genclerbirligi: 38 games
Antalyaspor: 28 games
Crystal Palace: 165 games
Aston Villa: 70 games

His Socceroos were still alive with a game to play in Russia, but their progress relied on a win over Peru and a Denmark loss to France to progress.

Peru, however, were too good. Andre Carrillo's 18th-minute goal was a delight.

Australia pushed. Rogic danced; Kruse surged; Mooy, Behich and Arzani tried their luck while Cahill was one decent Behich cross away from that precious sixth World Cup goal.

In the end, an era that promised so much ended with an anticlimax, a 2-0 defeat.

This chapter started with a young team taught to be brave, and to play the Australian way as the champions of the continent, but ended with another overseas coach, an underwhelming World Cup campaign, and another Australian football episode of 'what might have been'.

It really was the end of an era. No more Jedinak, Bresciano and Cahill. Soon, they would be joined by Robbie Kruse, a winger who fought back from so many injuries to serve his country so well. Later, Tom Rogic, a rare talent cherished by his club Celtic, and the only player to represent Australia in both football and futsal, also retired. Mark Milligan, one of our most versatile and committed Socceroos, led the side into the new era, but soon retired to focus on his coaching career.

A Miracle From Australia's Most-Loved Sporting Team

2019 FIFA Women's World Cup, France

If you looked into a crystal ball in January 2017 and saw that Ange Postecoglou and Alen Stajcic would *not* be coaching at the next World Cups, you'd have been laughed out of town!

But we told you at the start that this journey is full of highs, lows and everything in between. Neither men were at the 2018 and 2019 World Cups that they'd qualified for.

On the outside, the Matildas' form looked okay. Japan proved too good again in the Asian Cup final in April 2018, pipping the side via another late winner. Despite the Aussies dominating the ball, there was a surprising lack of oomph in front of goal, punished by the 84th-minute winning goal. Australia had twenty-three shots to five, but lost 1-0.

An 8-0 win over Vietnam aside, they did not win a game in normal time, but showed grit to claw back a group game draw against Japan, and they sent a semi-final against Thailand to penalties; Alanna Kennedy was the 90th-minute saviour.

August's Tournament of Nations also seemed productive. The Matildas were undefeated, but the USA claimed the trophy via goal difference.

"We genuinely believe we can (win the World Cup)," declared Alanna Kennedy, who scored a ridiculously good goal in a 2-0 win over Japan.

Against the USA, Chloe Logarzo's strike looked like a winner until Lindsey Horan's 90th-minute equaliser.

The public was still happy. Another 28,000 turned out for friendlies against Chile in Penrith and Newcastle.

On the park, a 5-0 win in Newcastle via a Foord treble, plus goals to Kerr and Emily Gielnik, was a relief. It came after a 3-2 loss three days earlier, plus a 2-0 loss to France and 1-1 draw with England in October.

Two months later, Football Australia sacked Stajcic.

It was five months away from the World Cup in France. They believed they had to move, quickly, to take the team in a new direction with fresh leadership and ideas.

It was a decision that strongly divided public opinion.

In the Matildas' recent history, the first few months of 2019 were the rockiest.

By March, Stajcic had bounced back, taking charge of A-League Men's side Central Coast. Since then, he has steered the Mariners from last to third in one season, took the Philippines' women's football side all the way to the 2022 Asian Cup semi-final and steered them to the 2023 Women's World Cup— their first ever—where they beat New Zealand *in* New Zealand. He currently coaches Western Sydney Wanderers in the A-League Men competition.

Stajcic dreamt of taking this group of Matildas to World Cup glory in 2019, but despite the controversial ending, his role, like Sermanni's, cannot be forgotten.

Ante Milicic, a prolific goal scorer in his day, and now a talented coach in charge of China's women's national side, was tasked with taking the Matildas to France, where expectations were high.

Every game of the tournament was being televised in Australia. In Europe, it felt like a wave, a women's football movement, was taking over.

Crowds were fabulous, the atmosphere world-class. Women's football had been led by Asia and North America, but suddenly the classic giants of football—European countries—had woken up. The USA won their fourth title, but times were changing. England, the Netherlands and Sweden made the semis; Norway, France, Italy and Germany were in the quarters.

It was a wake-up call for Asia, and Australia, but also an opportunity.

Suddenly, traditional football countries and their clubs were focusing on women's football as well.

Our own stars were about to experience a whole new world, a football fantasy that helped lift the Matildas.

LET'S GO SHOPPING: POST-WORLD CUP MOVES

Sam Kerr ⟶ Chelsea, 2019

Emily Gielnik ⟶ Bayern Munich, 2019

Caitlin Foord ⟶ Arsenal, 2020

Steph Catley ⟶ Arsenal, 2020

Lydia Williams ⟶ Arsenal, 2020

Ellie Carpenter ⟶ Lyon, 2020

Emily Van Egmond ⟶ West Ham, 2020

Hayley Raso ⟶ Everton, 2020

Chloe Logarzo ⟶ Bristol, 2020

Meanwhile, Australian coaches also started to move. Joe Montemurro (Arsenal, then Juventus and now Lyon) and Tanya Oxtoby (Chelsea assistant, now Northern Ireland boss) got great jobs.

The number of Aussies playing in England more than doubled by 2024.

At the 2019 Women's World Cup, the Matildas couldn't eclipse 2015's 'sudden-death' win, but they did produce another epic chapter, and a night no one watching will ever forget.

Just two games into the campaign, Milicic's Matildas were 45 minutes away from disaster. After so much hype, the Aussies were 2-0 down at half-time to Brazil, having started the tournament with a 2-1 defeat to Italy after copping a 95th-minute heartbreaker. *Le Azzurre* came back from 1-0 down, shocking the Matildas after Kerr gave Australia a 1-0 lead.

MATILDAS BEAT BRAZIL 3-2: THE MIRACLE OF MONTPELLIER

- Brazil hadn't lost a group game since 1995.
- Only ONCE in World Cup history had a team won from 2-0 down, also in 1995.
- Brazil had never blown a World Cup lead.
- Brazil hadn't conceded a group stage goal since 2003.

The Matildas came out and scored THREE TIMES in the second-half!

After defeat by Italy, the focus on the Matildas heated up. Women's football was starting to get a lot more attention, and that brought debate about games like the team had never really experienced before. Focus was at an all-time high. The pressure was on.

Talk about *NEVER SAY DIE.*

The Matildas produced one of the most astonishing performances in World Cup history. Stunning, and a brilliant response to the criticism.

It was a Brazil-Matildas game for the ages.

A NEW RIVALRY WITH A NEW DOMINANT FORCE

2000 Olympics: LOSS
2004 Olympics: LOSS
2007 World Cup: LOSS
2011 World Cup: LOSS
2015 World Cup: WIN
2016 Olympics: LOSS
2017 Tournament of Nations: WIN
2018 Tournament of Nations: WIN
2019 World Cup: WIN

Marta and Cristiane helped the South Americans to a lead despite lots of Matildas attacking play. It wasn't looking good.

Crucially, Foord scored just before the break. Game on.

"We knew we were in it at half-time," Kerr reflected.

On *SBS*, Steph Catley described the second-half as "an incredible showcase of skills from both teams".

Chloe Logarzo was *amazing.* She set up Foord, then scored the second with a shot through a crowded box.

Then, with the Matildas' momentum surging, Monica couldn't deal with van Egmond's lobbed ball into the box; her goalkeeper was stranded as the own goal floated past her and into the net. Brazil hoped the VAR would save them. We all waited anxiously as the VAR checked if an off-side Kerr got in the way.

GOAL. YES!!!
   44th minute: Down 2-0
   69th minute: Up 3-2

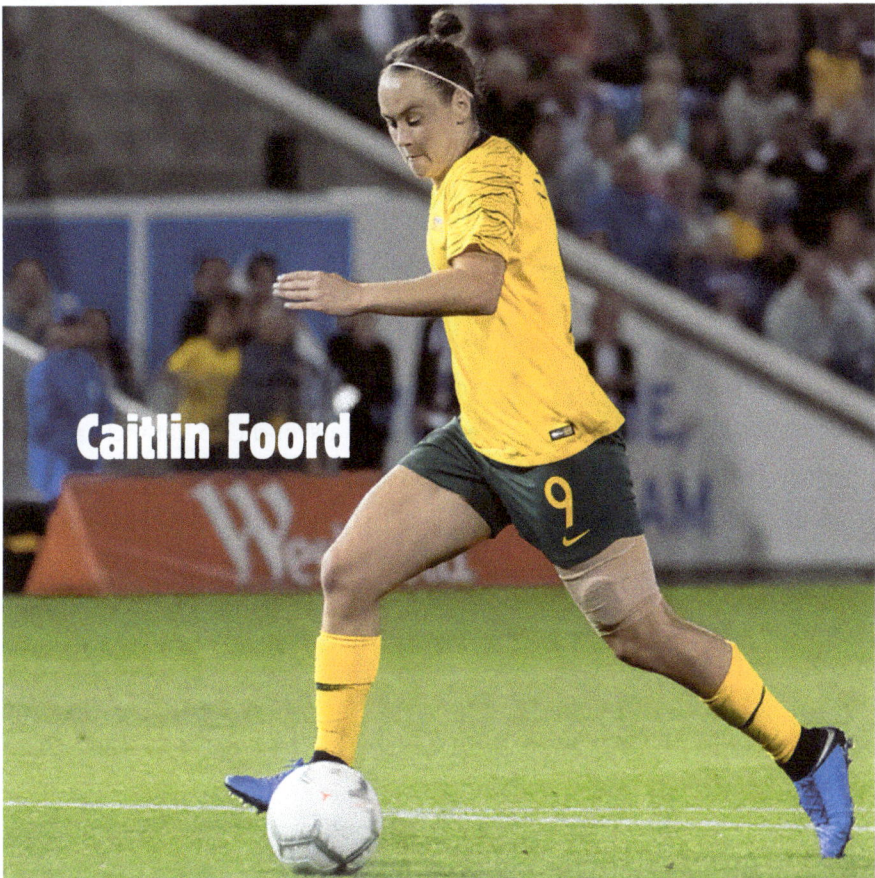

Caitlin Foord

A comeback for the ages!

How did that actually happen? Did it happen?

Never Say Die …

No one was more pumped than Kerr.

"There were a lot of critics talking about us," she said on TV after the game. "So suck on that."

The incredible result had the nation talking. Even the prime minister couldn't contain himself!

"Inspirational," Scott Morrison tweeted. "You never gave up."

Never Say Die.

There was still a crucial group game to play against Jamaica and a job to do. The thing about Kerr, who attracted more focus thanks to her post-match comments, is she always delivers when the stakes get higher.

Step up, skipper.
- ⚽ *11'*
- ⚽ *42'*
- ⚽ *69'*
- ⚽ *83'*

That's four goals in one World Cup match, thank you very much. She became the first Australian—male or female—to score a World Cup hat-trick, and just the third female ever to net four in one World Cup game!

"As an Australian football community, we should be thankful that we're witnessing one of the best players in the world, live," Milicic said, praising her afterwards.

It should be no surprise that when Europe's most famous clubs came calling from 2019-20, Kerr was the pin-up, and the first big-name Aussie to go. Her move after the tournament to Stamford Bridge to play for Chelsea made global headlines.

The blockbuster move took our local hero and ignited her journey to global icon.

A face for Nike. The front cover of EA Sports' *FIFA* game with Kylian Mbappe. The first Australian to be turned into LEGO.

Kerr had always been a gem at home, lighting up the W-League for home-town club Perth Glory and briefly with Sydney FC.

An Aussie female as a global star at an iconic football club: Kerr has turned a fantasy into a reality for Aussie kids.

"If I'm 18 years of age, it would be a dream to go and play for Chelsea. Years ago, people weren't thinking of going to England," explained Chloe Logarzo, talking about Kerr's impact in a chat with *News Corp.*

But that's Kerr.

Her story is one of breaking barriers and inspiring with her extra-special talent.

She's one of the rare sportspeople who can say their feats became iconic *moments.*

Her skills grew from a deeply talented sporting family—most famously, her brother Daniel won an AFL flag with the West Coast Eagles—and a growing love of football honed on the streets of Fremantle.

She was so fast when she was little that she didn't have to shoot— she would beat everyone to the goal first! She perfected her world-famous backflip on the school oval; just like any other kid, but with a super-human talent.

Amazingly, Kerr only started with a round ball at 12. Until then, she was obsessed with AFL.

By 15, she was playing for Australia.

THREE YEARS!!

Sermanni: "She was an extraordinary talent."

Stajcic: "It's abnormal that a person can run the ball that far at 13 against 15, 16-year-olds, who are the best in their state."

Milicic: "When I look back on my career, coaching her will be my greatest privilege."

God-given talent isn't enough, though. Plenty of talented athletes don't make it. Hard work, and then dealing with adversity, will always separate the best from the rest.

In December 2014, the clock started ticking on Kerr's 2015 World Cup dream after a crushing knee injury, one which usually puts athletes out for nine to twelve months.

Like everything in her career, she took the challenge on, and beat it to make it to the event in June 2015.

That determination on top of her talent has seen Kerr change football in Australia through the attention her performances and popularity have brought. She now stands alone, ahead of Timmy Cahill, as our nation's all-time international scorer.

Adored in equal measure by girls and boys, and mums and dads, fans love her skill.

They also recognise a very special quality: she keeps it real. A smile isn't ever too far away, even for such a fierce competitor. Socceroos' boss Graham Arnold once joked, "I wish I was allowed to select her for us!"

THE SAM KERR CV
Perth Glory (2008-11, 2014-2019)
Sydney FC (2012-14)
Western New York Flash (2013-14)
Sky Blue FC (2015-17)
Chicago Red Stars (2018-19)
Chelsea (2019-)

In France, Australia's World Cup campaign had been rescued by the epic win over Brazil, but penalty heartache would end it against Norway.

The European outfit took a 31st-minute lead in the Round of 16 but the Matildas pushed, and pushed, as you would expect.

With seven minutes to go, wow! Elise Kellond-Knight—KK—scored directly from a corner. An *Olimpico goal*, an incredibly rare thing to do, added another notch to KK's impressive World Cup resume, and gave the Aussies confidence heading into extra-time.

However, VAR luck was not on our side in this game. Two great penalty shouts were denied—for one, Kerr was so confident she had the ball ready on the penalty spot—before Kennedy was sent off for a professional foul.

Sam Kerr

Once it went down to penalties, well, it's a lottery. In Nice, both Gielnik and Kerr missed.

Some of the planet's biggest names have missed penalties. That's football. That's the World Cup. Anything can happen, even if you've just scored four goals in one game.

The exit was earlier than everyone hoped.

But in glimpses, the side showed its potential and didn't hurt the blossoming public love affair, with the Matildas named Australia's most-loved sporting team.

Caitlin Foord reflected, "It is heartbreaking. We came here to win the World Cup and the dream is over."

If only they knew. The dream was just beginning.

The Arnie Era: Mbappe and Messi Thanks to a Grey Wiggle

2022 FIFA World Cup, Qatar

Sport, the saying goes, is unscripted drama. The greatest plot you can follow for an adventure. So, when you take World Cup qualifying in Asia, throw in a global pandemic and the chaos of life in quarantine, you have the makings of a box-office thriller.

If Socceroos fans hoped for less stress getting to the 2022 World Cup in Qatar, well, sorry …

For the first time in a generation, there was a real and scary prospect that the World Cup might go ahead without us.

The quest for 2022 started smoothly enough on September 10, 2019 in Kuwait.

Who would have predicted we would be a Grey Wiggle shuffle from a horror ending on June 13, 2022, some 1008 days, 68 players and 16 away games later? The answer: NO ONE.

Remembering the players involved is like a trivia question.

Game 1, Australia v Kuwait: Mat Ryan, Rhyan Grant, Trent Sainsbury, Milos Degenek, Aziz Behich; Jackson Irvine, Aaron Mooy, James Jeggo; Mat Leckie, Adam Taggart, Brandon Borrello

Game 20, Australia v Peru: Mat Ryan; Nathaniel Atkinson, Bailey Wright, Kye Rowles, Aziz Behich; Aaron Mooy; Martin Boyle, Ajdin Hrustic, Jackson Irvine, Mat Leckie; Mitchell Duke

One man who was there for the whole journey was Graham Arnold. Like he's been there for Australian football for more than four decades.

Arnie.

Socceroo No. 334.

If you look closely enough at any Socceroos era since his debut in 1985, you'll likely spot Arnie in a picture.

He was there trying to qualify in '85, '89, '93 and '97, first as a young striker, 'goal-a-game Arnie', then the veteran desperate to end his curse. Images of him on the MCG turf in 1997 are infamously sad.

In 2001, he was Frank Farina's sidekick.

By 2005, he was alongside his new mentor Guus Hiddink.

He was thrown in the deep end in 2007, not yet ready to lead his country to the Asian Cup as coach, with some players who were once his teammates.

He took an Olyroos side to Beijing in 2008 where they faced Argentina and Lionel Messi at the Olympics—no Olyroos side would qualify again until Arnold returned in 2020.

He spent the next ten years away from the national team, but it was a decade that readied him for his return as he took fairy-tale club Central Coast to their first A-League championship, before backing that up with another championship with powerhouse side Sydney FC. By then, he'd done it all.

It was his time.

At 55 years of age, Arnie had two championships, three premierships and an Australian Cup in his cabinet, and had developed a roll call of talent at his clubs that he would reunite with in the national team.

ARNIE'S ROO-PRODUCTION LINE

Tom Rogic

Mat Ryan

Trent Sainsbury

Mitchell Duke

Mustafa Amini

Oliver Bozanic

Andrew Redmayne

Danny Vukovic

Rhyan Grant

Rivals of the Mariners and Sky Blues didn't love the appointment, but you cannot deny that Arnie bleeds green and gold, powered by a football beating in his heart.

Known now for being the wise head guiding our national team, Arnold was once a brilliant striker with a flowing mullet and questionable moustache, loved by Sydney Croatia in the National Soccer League, talented enough to be one of the first *Aussies Abroad* success stories. He was an early pioneer in the Netherlands, Belgium and Japan before returning home some 161 goals later. He is still highly respected in those countries.

By 2024, no one had coached Australia more times than Arnie.

Getting his beloved Socceroos to Qatar was what his career deserved. But it took its toll. It was a brutal journey.

His return wasn't entirely smooth, exiting the 2019 Asian Cup at the quarter-final stage after a 1-0 defeat to the United Arab Emirates.

Qualifying started routinely, with a group of players that made you feel safe: Ryan, Sainsbury, Behich, Irvine, Mooy, Leckie and Rogic.

Then, the world changed.

Life was thrown into chaos by COVID-19, and as the planet stopped, so too did football—especially because its huge crowds were seen as big risks.

Football moved carefully. The Socceroos would not meet again until 2021 in bubbles (groups kept together to avoid catching COVID from outside groups—remember that?) with empty stadiums in Kuwait and Qatar to squeeze all the Asian World Cup qualifying games in.

After a big win in Canberra in 2019, it would be **25 months** and **10 matches** until the boys came home, **763 days later**.

Being the Socceroos' boss is a very different gig.

You have challenges no one else on the planet really has to deal with. You scout your stars on the internet, then get them for a couple of sessions after they've arrived from all over the world, often travelling across the planet to get to a game.

Now, add in pandemic travel, quarantine, isolation and border shutdowns.

These were crazy days.

Four days out from playing Saudi Arabia in Sydney, five Socceroos were in Australia. Tactics? How about just getting players in to field a team!

Arnold was becoming a father figure, as much as he was a tactician. He decided to live abroad for seven months, leaving his wife, three kids and three grandkids in Australia. If he didn't, his days in isolation during travel would have added up to ninety-four! He caught the virus twice, too.

Arnold's dedication is the stuff of legend.

During this time, we met some fresh faces.

Riley McGree, a wonderful attacking talent; midfield options like Denis Genreau and Connor Metcalfe; winger Chris Ikonomidis and a confidence-boosted Mitchell Duke.

Arnie also knew his depth was skinny and needed bolstering.

With a magnifying glass and detective hat, he scouted Europe for players who could play for Australia through their family ties, but who were born overseas.

Who says you can't make signings in international football?

Harry Souttar, the 1.98-metre giant central defender, and Martin Boyle, the electric winger, were both Scottish-born, but pledged their futures to us. *Aussie, Aussie, Aussie!*

Arnold also secured playmaker Ajdin Hrustic, an Aussie who was eligible to play for Bosnia and Herzegovina if he accepted their invitations. Through these months, he emerged as Australia's most influential player—no surprise given he was in the Bundesliga in Germany at Eintracht Frankfurt.

Arnie also took the extra role of coaching the Olympics squad. It had been so long since we were last there.

Arnold was the coach in 2008 and retook control to get the side to Tokyo for the 2020 Games. They were an odd Olympics, delayed until 2021 due to the pandemic, and played in lockdown conditions.

Olympic football for men has been an under-23s tournament since 1992, with three overage players allowed, whereas for the women's competition, it is a full senior tournament.

Making the Olympics is a great boost for our young male players, giving them precious international experience, and it is a great place to get discovered.

Until our drought, our record was pretty good, too.

In our first home Olympics in 1956, which was a senior men's competition then, Australia came fifth. There was a quarter-final finish in 1988 in Seoul, South Korea—also with a senior men's team.

It is also worth knowing about Barcelona, in 1992, where the Olyroos finished fourth. Some of the names in that team ... wow!

Mark Bosnich. Ned Zelic. Aurelio Vidmar. Tony Popovic. Paul Okon. Steve Corica. Damian Mori. Carl Veart. Brad Maloney. John Markovski.

That is a Hall of Fame of Aussie skill, right there.

One of the most freakish goals ever scored in green and gold helped the Olyroos qualify for Barcelona.

Google 'Ned Zelic, Netherlands'. YouTube will do the rest. It is a goal few would even think of trying, let alone scoring.

Australia had to beat the Netherlands over two legs to qualify as Oceania's representative. After a 1-1 draw in Sydney, they went to Utrecht, with 'away goals' applying.

Down 2-1, twenty minutes into extra-time, Zelic produced a moment of genius from an impossible angle, squeezing a goal past a shocked goalkeeper. True *individual brilliance,* a phrase he made famous as a television pundit. Dare try that in your next game!

Zelic was a midfielder in an era that had a celebrated number of players with flair and a natural love of the ball, developed from hours on the park, in the street, in backyards or patches of grass at home, mastering touch and technique. It was all through a love of the outdoors. There were no devices or phones for afterschool entertainment. Touch. Touch. Touch. Touch. Pass. Pass. Pass. Pass. It created a rare group of footballers.

Tokyo was the next chapter. Why are we including it here? Because against Argentina (South American champions), Egypt (Africa champions) and Spain (European champions), the core of our World Cup and Asian Cup squad was on trial. When the World Cup arrived, they benefited from having an international tournament under their belt.

- Nathaniel Atkinson
- Keanu Baccus
- Thomas Deng
- Joel King
- Riley McGree
- Connor Metcalfe
- Kye Rowles
- Harry Souttar
- Cam Devlin
- Marco Tilio

Marco Tilio scored the goal of his life from outside the box—a first-time strike caressed gloriously into the side of the net—to shock Argentina in a 2-0 opening win. Joel King set up Lachie Wales for the other goal. Tight losses against Spain (0-1) and Egypt (0-2) ended the dream.

Marco Tilio

Rowles is an especially nice story. At this point, he was a little-known Central Coast defender. In the coming months, he would get thrown in the deep end and thrive in the World Cup play-offs, and never look back.

Give the kids a go, you never know …

It is hard to believe this side came so close to missing out on Qatar, because by October 2021, they were in control and it was a good story.

They even set a WORLD RECORD, becoming the first side in world football to **win eleven straight World Cup qualifiers in one campaign.**

THE WORLD RECORD

Kuwait 3-0, Kuwait City
Nepal 5-0, Canberra
Taiwan 7-1, Kaohsiung
Jordan 1-0, Amman
Kuwait 3-0, Kuwait City
Chinese Taipei 5-1, Kuwait City
Nepal 3-0, Kuwait City
Jordan 1-0, Kuwait City
China 3-0, Doha
Vietnam 1-0, Doha
Oman 3-1, Doha

QUALIFYING GOES WRONG

Then, gulp. History repeated. Enter Japan and Saudi Arabia, like in 2017.

Japan 1-2, Saitama
Saudi Arabia 0-0, Sydney

One month after the world record, sealed in a 3-1 win over Oman in Qatar, the campaign was quickly in trouble. Like in 2017, pressure piled up. Critics grew louder. COVID rules made things terribly tricky.

China 1-1, Sharjah

Vietnam 4-0, Melbourne

Oman 2-2, Muscat

Japan 0-2, Sydney

Saudi Arabia 0-1, Jeddah

L. D. D. W. D. L. L. Aaaaarrgggh.

The struggle streak after the winning streak.

It all threatened to fall apart in 2022. At this moment, the Socceroos were not good enough, and Arnie's job was under threat.

Back to the dreaded play-offs.

In June 2022, anyone 16 years or younger was staring down the barrel of a first World Cup without Australia in their lives.

Against Uruguay in 2005, it felt like our time.

Against Honduras in 2017, we were simply a better team.

In 2022, we had to play the United Arab Emirates and Peru in one-off games at a neutral venue (not two legs home and away like in previous years). UAE had knocked us out of the Asian Cup, and the South Americans were ranked 22 in the world, 20 places ahead of us.

Hmmmmm, it wasn't looking good.

Football will always be played and enjoyed in Australia, even if we are not at World Cups. But being there makes it so much more exciting: the whole country stops for our sport. It is the best window for fans, like you, to fall in love with the football world.

How big were the stakes in 2022?

In Arnie's words, "I was one kick away from being Australia's most hated man!"

Play-offs can be described as a flip of the coin, but Australia wanted to ensure that our games against the UAE and Peru weren't going to come down to luck in 2022. Our preparation was better.

Wisely, Arnie insisted on a friendly against Jordan one week before the UAE play-off to get used to the air-conditioned stadium in Qatar. He realised that the air-conditioning impacted the speed of the ball on the pitch and knew it was an advantage.

The Socceroos were too good for the UAE, but they made us sweat.

In the 53rd-minute, Boyle surged down the right to tee up Irvine after a classy late run from midfield into the box, but the UAE levelled just three minutes later after sloppy defending in the box.

It couldn't happen, could it?

With seven minutes to go, one moment could swing everything: would it be a moment of quality, or a mistake?

Step up, Hrustic. Quality, it would be.

If you don't try your luck, you'll never know what might have been.

The classy midfielder unleashed a gutsy volley through a crowded box to score the winner in a 2-1 triumph. Phew.

Next up, Peru. This game would decide the final spot available at the 2022 World Cup in December in six months' time.

The South Americans, who beat Australia 2-0 in Russia, were fifth in qualifying behind Argentina, Brazil, Uruguay and Ecuador. We know all too well from our Uruguay and Argentina experiences how much qualifying for a World Cup means to these nations. They even brought 15,000 travelling fans with them to Doha.

Arnie used that to fire up his side.

"We like being (the) underdog," he insisted. "We like people saying we have no chance."

He was there in 2005. "This game (is) alongside that," he explained. "It is a life-changing moment for these boys."

How right that comment would prove to be.

Football might be a religion in South America, but prayers can only take you so far. Australia was better prepared in Doha, and it showed: well-structured, hungry and focused.

Peru had just one shot on target in a nerve and tension-filled match.

But those 120 minutes became the entrée to an unexpected main course.

When it looked like both teams couldn't be split, Arnie made the biggest gamble of his life in the 120th minute.

OFF: Australia's captain Mat Ryan

ON: Sydney FC goalkeeper Andrew Redmayne

I can still remember the flood of early morning texts that hit my phone as Arnold rolled the dice.

Was he mad?

Is he serious?

Oh my goodness!

WHAT WAS HE DOING?!

Playing mind games, that's what.

Remember, seventeen years earlier, how Kalac was warming up to replace Schwarzer? It was a trick from Hiddink that Arnold had kept up his sleeve for all these years.

He isn't the first person to try it. Another famous Netherlands coach Louis van Gaal did it in the 2014 World Cup quarter-final, and it worked.

But for a place at the World Cup?

WOW!

That takes some serious guts.

"(Peru) spent the whole week preparing for Maty being in goal," Redmayne explained, modestly. "Putting me there instead threw them a little bit."

Arnie added, "I'd been planning this for weeks. They'd never seen Redmayne before!"

Imagine what the Peruvians were thinking: *If they've just taken off their captain and brought on a bearded, older guy who looks like a bushranger, he must be a weapon at penalties!*

Sport, and the mind, can do funny things.

Redmayne had successfully performed his dancing jig in the 2019 A-League Grand Final when Sydney won in Perth, but if Peru's coaches quickly Googled his record, they'd have found:

- He'd saved 4/31 career penalties.

- It was just his third Socceroos game at 33 years of age.

- He was rescued by Arnie at Sydney, as he was thinking of retiring after a journey through Brisbane, the Central Coast, Melbourne City and Western Sydney. He had even done a barista course, and was studying teaching at university, planning for life outside of football.

Arnie just had a hunch and backed himself.

After everything he'd done for Australia, he didn't deserve this gamble to backfire.

He looked towards the sky and whispered, "Please, Mum."

The Grey Wiggle strode out. Chest puffed. Beard flowing intimidatingly.

His coach had bet his career on him. A nation held its breath.

The world looked on in disbelief.

IS HE … HE'S NOT?

DANCING?

Or is he waving? Wait, he IS actually dancing AND waving! What is going on?!

The Socceroos showed nerves of steel, especially once Boyle missed the opening spot-kick.

Mooy, Goodwin, Hrustic, Maclaren and Mabil were HUGE.

Redmayne, one of the sport's nice guys, discovered a water bottle with Peru's notes on Australia's penalty takers. No more Mr Nice Guy.

Secretly, he tossed it over the fence while goalkeeper Pedro Gallese wasn't looking.

Whatever it takes.

Then, with a wiggle, a wave, a crouch and a stare, Redmayne produced the most famous save Australia had seen since Mark Schwarzer's in 2005.

The Socceroos defeated Peru 5-4 on penalties.

WORLD CUP, HERE WE COME!

All Redmayne could do was stand and smile, a special pose for his daughter watching back home.

Then, he was mobbed and his life changed forever.

As Australian football fans celebrated and breathed a sigh of relief at the same time, the internet lost its mind over Redmayne's antics. A humble A-League star had become an Australian sensation. The football world could not believe his antics.

His dancing routine even earned an invitation from The Wiggles to

Andrew Redmayne with Craig Goodwin
in the changing room after the match

become the honorary Grey Wiggle.

Redmayne's response was typical of the owner of Australia's newest iconic sporting moment.

"I'm no hero."

This team, a collective, might not have the *individual* heroes of yesteryear, but this was the start of becoming a Socceroos *team* to be admired.

Redmayne represented so much of the best of the side, with his qualities of never giving up.

Ryan's humility, when many would have been furious at being substituted, is the measure of the man. What a leader. Mooy, meanwhile, produced one of the games of his life, after hardly playing club football in China all year.

For the man who brought them together, his tactic was no longer madness, but viewed as genius.

The result brought him to tears.

"Colin" was the first person he wanted to thank on Network 10, his older brother who had been his shining star when he'd lost both his parents before he was 25 years of age.

Resilience learnt from those tough moments in life was how he made it through a qualifying campaign many would not have.

He turned the Socceroos into a family.

When he finally got his reward, the first thing he thought of was his own family.

Everything about the 2022 World Cup was different: it was the first in the Middle East, and the first in December, the middle of the club season. As the last side to qualify, there were only six months for the Socceroos until the World Cup, held in the same place as our play-off.

On the park, the football was insane, and Australia played its part.

It is hard not getting goose bumps thinking about Australia's tournament, a World Cup beyond anyone's wildest imagination. An incredible adventure.

It was proof that a *team* united and with a shared bond—a love of Australia and each other—can do wonderful things, even if it doesn't boast the world's biggest names. Or, indeed, not even the biggest names in its own country's history.

After Arnold's Peru risk-taking, his twenty-six-man World Cup squad also included surprises.

Souttar had hardly played in a year after a devastating knee injury.

Rowles had been out injured for six weeks.

Eight players were chosen from the A-League.

Loveable Mariners striker Jason Cummings, another player scouted and poached from Scotland, surged into the squad thanks to his form in the A-League. The Central Coast striker was there for his goals, but also his gags. He had become a fan favourite in Australia.

His clubmate Garang Kuol was also in at just 18 years of age. A bolter, like Arzani four years ago. The teenager was fearless, fast and in form. The future of Australia was the present. If you're good enough, then you're old enough.

Those two picks were remarkable. One year earlier, Kuol was still in Victoria's National Premier League second division. Cummings was on the bench for Dundee, the worst club in the Scottish Premier League at the time.

Get your chance, take it. Not happy, change it. Take risks. Back yourself.

Know your talent. These two, one 18 years old, the other 27, showed that in 2022.

If we thought Peru was the high point of the 2022 campaign, we were so very wrong. It was just the lottery ticket to Group D.

Arnold, before the World Cup: "We want to create the greatest Socceroos team ever."

But let's be honest: beforehand, we thought that was a pipedream. Expectations were not high.

France: World champions. Kylian Mbappe. Antoine Griezmann. Olivier Giroud. Ousmane Dembele. Hugo Lloris. Depth so good they could name two or three teams.

Tunisia: African side ranked 35th in the world.

Denmark: World No. 11, fresh off a Euro 2020 semi-final, and full of Premier League stars like Christian Eriksen and Kasper Schmeichel.

Could the Socceroos do something special? As it got closer to kick-off and the squad spent a rare amount of quality time together, a quiet confidence, and steely resolve, was starting to grow around the camp.

What happened next will go down in Australian sporting folklore.

SOCCEROOS FIRSTS

1. *Back-to-back World Cup wins*
2. *Two World Cup wins in one tournament*
3. *Back-to-back clean sheets*
4. *Most points ever at a World Cup*
5. *First win in twelve years*
6. *A goal in every game*
7. *Australia led every group game 1-0*
8. *Arnold the first Aussie to coach a knockout-stage game*
9. *Garang Kuol became the youngest player in a knockout game since Pele in 1958*
10. *Final finish: 11th*

As the Socceroos' momentum built, December 2022 also proved that we are a true football nation.

In fact, we're a MAD football nation.

Thanks to social media, the watching world could not believe the scenes at 3:00 a.m. across the country, especially at Federation Square in Melbourne, which was packed with buzzing football fans.

Australia always unites for big sporting events, and every four years, football's bandwagon bursts. Everyone's welcome!

This was another level, though. By the Round of 16, stadiums were being sold out just to watch a giant television screen. BEFORE DAWN!

No sport—in fact, almost nothing else—can unite Australia, from coast to coast, young to old, boy or girl, fanatic or not, like football.

You can love AFL, NRL, cricket, Olympic sports, tennis, golf or whatever is your passion. That's the beauty of our sunburnt country. There is so much sport for us to enjoy.

Nothing is as exotic, dramatic or global as football, though. It is the one true window to the world, and the world's window to us.

Fourteen million people in France watched their opening-night win over the Socceroos.

That's fourteen million who were stunned when two local A-League players combined to shock the defending champions to take a 1-0 lead.

La surprise!

It was part excitement, part sheer disbelief when the Aussies took a lead thanks to scintillating play between Mathew Leckie and Craig Goodwin.

The Melbourne City star surged down the right flank before an inch- perfect cross found Adelaide United's captain flying down the left, ready to seize his moment with a fearless finish past Hugo Lloris.

Breathtaking.

Arnold's side started with true belief and it paid off; Australians went wild in the stands as Goodwin slid to the corner flag, after taking a moment to look skywards to remember and acknowledge his grandma in the biggest moment of his career.

"In those moments, you are kind of just that little boy that's in your backyard … dreaming of those moments," Goodwin said.

This book is full of different stories and journeys that might just become yours. Goodwin, a World Cup debutant at 31, was still working at KFC when he made his pro debut ten years earlier, which was not long after he wasn't even making South Australian youth squads.

Now, he's a World Cup goal scorer. Not only a reward for a life's work, but for six months battling back from injury to make it to Qatar.

France's squad was worth $1.66 billion. Ours? $59 million.

I'll never forget the joy of going 1-0 up. That's what an Aussie side does—it has a go. In years to come, let's aim to have the quality to match a big nation—and with that style—for 90 minutes, not just being content with great moments like these.

It was unsurprising that the opening goal triggered *Les Bleus* into life. They were one mighty team.

Juventus' Adrien Rabiot levelled just five minutes later, before he set up Olivier Giroud (AC Milan). Mbappe was starting to put on a show, his acceleration like nothing our defenders had experienced before. He opened his account in the second-half, before chipping to Giroud for a ruthless fourth.

The Socceroos had two close moments: a Duke blast and Irvine header when still 2-1. In the end it was as simple as: too good, overpowered, outclassed.

Criticism of the four-goal collapse followed, especially as four years earlier at the World Cup in Russia, it was a tighter 2-1 final score.

What those critics couldn't measure was the incredible bond and belief within this band of brothers. The next two games were the ones that would define the team's tournament.

The squad learnt from their coach, who had battled pressure for four years. Indeed, for his whole career.

His skipper, Maty Ryan, said, "It's all about how you deal with it and how resilient you are."

And Arnie has been nothing but resilient.

Game two, Tunisia at Al Janoub Stadium, felt like a Tunisia home game. It was so loud, the whistling was deafening. It was a hostile setting for a must-win game.

What's the best way to silence a noisy crowd?

Ask Mitchell Duke.

Twenty-three minutes into a tense, gripping contest, Goodwin crossed from the left and the striker somehow adjusted his body to glance home what proved to be the winning goal.

That was one for the true believers, a reward for Arnold's faith in Duke, a No. 9 who was playing in Japan's second division.

Any doubters were now quiet. In Qatar, he was spectacular. Hard-working. Quality from the front. Confident. You don't need to be fashionable to succeed, just block out the critics.

The 31-year-old sprinted off and kept a promise to his little boy, melting hearts, showing the world a celebration they designed together.

"One of the highlights of my career," he beamed. "The best feeling in the world."

Duke's goal got the attention. However, Souttar made a tackle as good as a goal to keep it at 1-0.

With the Africans pushing, and four minutes left, they surged into the open and Aussie hearts sank.

We should not have been worried; we had Big Harry Souttar!

The tallest man in the tournament, who only played 90 senior club minutes that season returning from injury before the World Cup, flew like an Olympic gold medal sprinter to mow down the attack.

Arnold spoke regularly about the side's Aussie DNA—a *backs-against-the-wall*, underdog mindset. Maybe it was true, after all? With the pressure rising, so too did the Aussies.

SOUTTAR v TUNISIA

100% OF TACKLES WON
100% OF GROUND DUELS WON

For the first time since 2010, Australia celebrated three points in a World Cup game and there could not have been a more fitting scorer than Duke to reflect the *team* and culture being built.

In 2010, we could call on Cahill, Bresciano, Holman or Kewell. In 2024, our attack came from Adelaide United, Melbourne City, Central Coast,

Cadiz and Fagiano Okayama. Arnold needed this group to *believe,* and to believe *together.*

In Duke, he had a warrior up front. He backed him, and the striker repaid his coach with the crowning moment of his career.

You might hear the phrase of strikers *leading the line.* Duke simply led the way for his country at this World Cup, bringing energy, touch, power and belief. He was thrown into the Socceroos in 2013, and then was out of the picture until 2019, while bouncing between the A-League, Japan and Saudi Arabia.

Perseverance.

Just how big was his performance? On November 26, 2022, four players were presented with World Cup man-of-the-match awards.

1. Robert Lewandowski (Poland 2, Saudi Arabia 0)
2. Kylian Mbappe (France 2, Denmark 1)
3. Lionel Messi (Argentina 2, Mexico 0)
4. Mitchell Duke (Australia 1, Tunisia 0)

No more words are needed.

As Australians partied in the stands and at public gatherings back home, defender Milos Degenek sat on the bench in tears.

His head in his hands, these were tears of happiness.

"Life is the most beautiful thing," he tweeted. "From absolutely nothing to winning a World Cup game. Representing the country that gave me everything. THANK YOU SOCCEROOS. NEVER STOP BELIEVING IN YOURSELF."

Our football teams showcase the best of our country.

They unify us; their response to highs and lows teach and inspire us.

Degenek, for example, spoke beautifully during the World Cup about perspective and gratefulness.

"Pressure is me as a baby fleeing a war," he said. "Pressure is not 'I must win a football game!'"

Nine of the 2022 squad were born overseas. We had our Scottish trio.

There was an inspiring, growing African influence, with Thomas Deng, Awer Mabil and Garang Kuol becoming role models for their communities.

The three players are the first Socceroos with South Sudanese origin and all arrived in Australia as refugees. They enjoy their special bond together as much as they relish their status as role models at such a young age.

"Being able to represent different heritages and being that role model to many kids and to show them that hard work leads to you getting somewhere—I think it's something that I hold close to me," Kuol said.

"I want to prove to kids, especially South Sudanese kids around the world, that you can make something of yourself."

Australia is at its best when it embraces its multiculturalism; so too is our football team.

The Socceroos showcase the best side of our nation. As Awer Mabil says, "Many journeys, one journey."

Deng: "No matter what background you are from, as long as you work hard, opportunities will be given."

The next opportunity? Denmark.

Those old enough to remember Stuttgart in 2006 remember the Socceroos' final group game with Croatia like a grand final.

The looming clash with Denmark was this generation's *Croatia moment.* Pressure on the European outfit was intense, and Arnold's side quietly sensed a massive opportunity. But they would have to be at their very best.

Strap yourselves in.

It was 2:00 a.m. back home but a nation was gripped.

Denmark started well, looking every part the world's tenth-best side. But as the Socceroos eased into the game, their confidence grew. It was massive to go into break still at 0-0.

Keanu Baccus came on at half-time to add steel to the midfield and he helped the mightily impressive Jackson Irvine, Aaron Mooy and Riley McGree to express themselves.

That trio had superb World Cups; for Mooy, back in Europe with Ange Postecoglou at Celtic in Scotland after a hard stint in China that stalled his career, he reminded everyone why he was a Premier League player.

Known as the Pasty Pirlo, an affectionate nickname comparing him to Italian maestro Andrea Pirlo, Mooy is another role model for those who suffer setbacks.

He knew his quality; so, after braving it out at St Mirren in Scotland from 2010-2012, he came home, but did not play much at Western Sydney. He regrouped and became *so good* at Melbourne City that Manchester City bought him, loaning him to Brighton, and then Huddersfield. It was the long route, but it was his unique journey. And you don't play one hundred and forty-two Premier League games unless you're top class, and few modern Socceroos have struck a ball as purely as Mooy.

Qatar was his stage to showcase, once and for all, how good he was.

With Mooy pulling the strings, Al Janoub Stadium felt a swing in momentum.

Fifteen minutes into the second-half, Duke won the ball deep in Australia's own half. He found McGree who looked up, summed up his options, and played a clever direct pass into space to push Australia forward.

Mathew Leckie sprinted forward to collect it. He surged. He twisted. He turned. Surely Denmark had him covered. Wait a minute, he couldn't score, could he?

He might score!

SHOOT.

He DID shoot. He SCORED. MAT LECKIE!

Oh my goodness!

Australia 1. Denmark 0.

Speed. Skill. Smarts. Leckie left Joachim Maehle and a surprised Kasper Schmeichel for dead, surprising them by taking an early, left-foot strike, placed to perfection across the keeper and into the goal.

As he ran to his teammates, thumping the crest on his chest, Leckie wrote his name into Australian football folklore.

Harry Kewell, the golden boy in 2006.

Mathew Leckie, the hero in 2022.

The ultimate comparison for any Australian winger.

"A legend," declared his captain, before describing Leckie as "an absolute beast".

Mathew Leckie

The timing of the goal was perfect. Just seconds beforehand, Tunisia took the lead against France, knocking Australia down to third on the live table. Leckie's goal put the Socceroos back into second place.

Leckie was fed expertly by McGree, a talent backed by Arnold who had a really good World Cup. At 24, he was starting to live up to his potential, establishing himself in England's Championship with Birmingham, before moving to Middlesbrough after the World Cup. If you haven't seen it before, search for his 2018 A-League finals goal for Newcastle Jets. His 'scorpion' is the most freakish goal in the competition's history and earned him a Puskas Award nomination for world football goal of the year in 2018, which was won by a fella called Mohamed Salah.

Finally, the spotlight was on Leckie, which his underrated career deserved.

Not many Aussies play in the Bundesliga, Germany's top division. Leckie did so one hundred and fifty times.

Underappreciated, no more.

Denmark had quality all over the park but the Aussies stood tall; there was still 30 minutes plus six agonising minutes of added time to negotiate, but Australia outplayed the World No. 10.

Utter happiness spilled at the full-time whistle. The team huddled proudly on the field, sharing this special moment together.

The Socceroos took the final place available in Qatar. Their squad was dismissed as a shadow of former Australian sides. Now, they were into the final sixteen for the first time since 2006.

After the game, Irvine was shown videos from the celebrations back home. It reminded him of his own childhood.

"I hope every single one of them has a night they'll remember for the rest of their lives," he said proudly. "Like I've had as a fan as well."

Irvine was there against Uruguay in 2005. His mum took him out of school and they flew to Sydney for the game. He was in the stands with his family in Germany, 2006, as well.

"A fan became a player," he wrote for *Fox Sports* in 2017. "Simple as that."

Many in this group were 10 years of age when their heroes beat Uruguay —at the start of this book—and made the 2006 Round of 16.

He added an amazing message: "Any young aspiring Socceroos at the ground, or watching on television … it is possible to live your dream."

After the celebrations, we all stopped for a moment to make sure it was real.

Just six months earlier, the side was one Wiggles dance away from becoming a meme.

Belief. Togetherness. Determination. Underappreciated players. An inspiring coach.

Mabil pointed to Martin Boyle for the best explanation behind this amazing story.

The winger was ruled out of the World Cup on the eve of the tournament, but stayed, on crutches, to show his support.

Look closely at pictures of the team in a huddle on the park after the Denmark win, and there's Boyle, in the middle.

"It just shows the family we have," Mabil said. "So many people doubted us but we have stuck together."

Suddenly, surprisingly and sensationally, Australia was in the World Cup Round of 16 against Argentina.

Smells like team spirit: Martin Boyle with Graham Arnold in the middle of the Socceroos' World Cup huddle celebrating a win in Qatar

The Qatar World Cup had turned into the *Messi World Cup*, the icon's quest to finally guide his nation to the Holy Grail and end, once and for all, the G.O.A.T debate. It's a quest that stops a nation, literally, when the national team plays.

Could the Socceroos play the role of party pooper?

Australia. Argentina. World Cup knockout. You had to repeat it over and over to believe it was actually happening. You simply could not find a spare ticket to this match. The stakes, and stage, were massive.

In the USA, six million people tuned in. They came for Messi, of course, but got a healthy look at a gutsy Socceroos.

At 2:00 a.m. at home, a million diehard fans were glued to *SBS*. Across the country, live sites were packed, painting a sea of gold.

In Doha, the Al Janoub Stadium could have been *La Bombonera* in Buenos Aires, the home of Boca Juniors. Argentina fans travel, they sing their hearts out. Every game is a home match.

For 34 minutes, the Socceroos impressed and shut out the noise. Arnie's men even started to play some nice football.

And just when they did, they committed football's biggest sin: upsetting Lionel Messi.

It was the turning point.

Aziz Behich, who had enjoyed an unbelievable World Cup at left-back, confronted Messi on the touchline and a scuffle ignited.

It lit a fuse.

If it was NRL or AFL, fans would be yahooing. *You beauty! Go you good thing, get in there, boys!*

No, no, no. Not in football. YOU DON'T PROVOKE A GOAT!

Messi had been contained until then.

All it took was a split second.

Almost immediately, Nicolas Otamendi's touch fell to his captain on the right side of the field. That was good fortune. The rest was divine.

A shimmy and a rapid shot later, Messi was wheeling off to celebrate a goal in his thousandth professional game. What just happened?

Greatness.

The Socceroos composed themselves and continued to compete but

Graham Arnold with the squad for the 2022 FIFA World Cup

disaster struck on the hour when Manchester City talent Julio Alvarez pounced on a rare Mat Ryan error.

2-0 should've been job done, but not with this Aussie outfit. They showed the world their ticker. And quality.

Argentina were made to *sweat*, as the final exchanges became a big part of *La Albiceleste's* World Cup story.

Craig Goodwin, on as a sub, tried his luck from distance and a deflection helped us back into the game.

Then chaos! Drama! End-to-end breathlessness! You didn't know whether to look or close your eyes.

What incredible character from the Socceroos, where lesser sides would have collapsed.

This was classic World Cup football, what an advertisement for the sport: a minnow going toe-to-toe with the eventual champions. Ninety minutes of highs and lows. If you weren't already a football fan, how could you not be after watching this?

For 20 crazy minutes, the comeback was on. Oh. My. God. It was really on.

Behich charged down the left, cut inside, slalomed like he was skiing, kept going, wound up, shot …

WE COULD ALL SEE THE BALL ABOUT TO HIT THE BACK OF THE NET but out of nowhere, Manchester United's Lisandro Martinez lunged with a block so perfect defenders should worship it in a gallery.

Then Kuol, the baby of the tournament, turned and shot in space in the box. Time stood still until Emi Martinez, Argentina's goalkeeper, produced a huge save.

Martinez, also Aston Villa's keeper, went on to become the penalty hero in the World Cup final against France (coincidentally, the two teams that beat Australia in Qatar). He only got that chance because of his heroics in the Round of 16 against the Socceroos.

Argentina celebrated. Australia slumped.

Inspiring a new generation of Socceroos:

Thomas Deng, Garang Kuol and Awer Mabil

There was sadness to be going home. But there was pride in what we'd shown the world; in what we'd shown our own nation, both on and off the park.

Take Mat Ryan as an example.

What makes Ryan a cut above is his leadership, humility and sportsmanship. He didn't rebel when Redmayne replaced him against Peru; and he owned his mistake against Argentina, going on to make further saves in the same game. How would you have reacted in those moments? How we react to a challenge always says a lot about us.

Soon, the No. 1 will take over as our most-capped Socceroo. Not bad for a kid from the Mariners, once a shy teenager playing first-team football, who worked his way from Gosford to the Premier League, even playing for Arsenal, the club he supported as a boy. He has also tasted European club football with stints in Belgium, Spain, the Netherlands, Denmark and Italy. After so much doubt, even negativity, the Socceroos under Ryan's leadership had matched their own heroes, and in some records, even gone past them.

Like in 2006, it took the eventual champions to eliminate the Australians.

Off the park, it united a nation of sports-loving fans. We got a taste, again, of the power of the beautiful game.

On the park, this was genuinely a classic Australian underdog story.

But for the sport to truly go to the next level, making the Round of 16 should not be the high point as Australian football looks to continue to improve and grow in all aspects on and off the park, building on the dream.

"I'm sick of being the underdog," Arnie told *FIFA* in 2024.

"I'm sick of people coming over to me and saying, 'Jeez, you boys played well against England, god you were unlucky'...

"I'm sick of it.

"I want the day to come when people say, 'Jeez, it was so good to see you beat England' or those other nations that are ahead of us."

Amen to that.

The Greatest Month in Australian Football History

2023 FIFA Women's World Cup, Australia and New Zealand

If there are two hundred and eleven national associations in FIFA, then on June 26, 2020, the biggest story in two hundred and nine of them was Liverpool finally winning their first Premier League trophy.

But in Australia and New Zealand, an announcement was made that would change everything for the sport in the two countries.

WE ARE GOING TO HOST A FIFA WORLD CUP!

The bid was chosen by FIFA's panel with twenty-two votes against Colombia's thirteen. With women's football's incredible growth, it was a great time to host the tournament.

The next big news story was the appointment of Tony Gustavsson—Tony G—who landed one of the biggest jobs in Australian sport's history as the new coach of the Matildas. The Swede's to-do-list, in charge of a Golden Generation of talent, was of historical scale:

1. 2020 Olympic Games
2. 2022 Asian Cup
3. 2023 Women's World Cup on home soil
4. 2024 Olympics

Fortunately, he came with quite the CV, headlined by being the assistant coach of the US women's team as they won the 2015 and 2019 World Cups.

It wasn't an easy start. COVID meant the Tillies did not see each other for three hundred and ninety-five days across 2020 and 2021. He started with 5-2 and 5-0 losses to Germany and the Netherlands in friendly matches ahead of the COVID-delayed Tokyo Olympics in 2021.

But thankfully in Tokyo, the side finally pushed into the last four of a major tournament, making the semis.

"Belief," Kerr said about what their new boss had added as they enjoyed their best ever result at a global tournament.

It was a hurdle the Matildas wanted—needed—to jump. A historical bucket list.

OLYMPIC CAMPAIGN
New Zealand, 2-1 win
Sweden, 2-4 loss
USA, 0-0 draw
Great Britain, 4-3 win in extra-time
Sweden, 0-1 loss
USA, 3-4 loss

The Olympic fortnight unleashed two teenagers who hinted they would be key Matildas, quickly. Mary Fowler and Kyra Cooney-Cross looked like two sublimely talented players, comfortable already at this level. We also celebrated an Olympic debut for Aivi Luik at 36 years of age and welcomed Kyah Simon back from injury.

The front three were electric: Foord, Kerr and Simon.

After navigating the group stage, the quarter-final triumph over Team GB was gripping. Kennedy enjoyed Olympic redemption after the pain of missing a penalty in the shootout against Brazil in Rio, heading home the opener. GB had been on top, but keeper Tegan Micah was on fire.

With just two minutes left, GB led 2-1.

Never Say Die, eh. It's not just a tagline. This side just doesn't know when the game is over.

It was Kerr, of course.

Big stage. BIG PLAYER. She did it all herself, whacking home the equaliser.

Sheer talent and desire.

Micah spectacularly saved a penalty in extra-time and a mere two minutes later, Fowler wound up from distance and a deflection helped her strike home.

Kerr headed the Aussies 4-2 ahead; then Ellen White's hat-trick set up a nervous five minutes at 4-3, but the victory was Australia's.

"I will never forget the feeling," Gustavsson raved.

A tough 1-0 loss to Sweden was followed by a 4-3 defeat to the USA.

Kerr became the side's all-time top scorer with her 48th goal for her country, and Emily Gielnik scored from so far out that few would have even dared to try it, let alone been able to score it.

There were still two years until the World Cup, but something special was bubbling away. Australia, with Olympic fever mixed in, fell for the Matildas.

The two million who tuned in for the semi-final made it the most watched women's team sport match ever in Australia.

The starting XI for the semi-final vs England
Back (L-R): Ellie Carpenter, Kyra Cooney-Cross, Mary Fowler, Clare Hunt, Mackenzie Arnold, Clare Polkinghorne, Katrina Gorry.
Front (L-R): Hayley Raso, Steph Catley, Sam Kerr (c), Caitlin Foord

Mary Fowler

At a tournament where a cauldron shines brightly, a flame had been lit for Australia and the Tillies.

"We feel the love from home," Kerr said.

Gustavsson: "You can win trophies. And you can win the *hearts of the people.*"

🏀

Unfortunately, it wasn't as rosy by January 2022 when the side failed at the Asian Cup in India where they were the top-ranked nation. South Korea defeated the Matildas 1-0 in the quarter-finals.

Not even an 18-0 win over Indonesia in the group stage, which Australia otherwise scratched through, silenced the critics. In fact, they worried that games like that should have been used to play some of the kids, without captain Kerr, to test them out in case she was ever injured.

18-GOAL FEAST

Five: Kerr

Three: van Egmond

Two: Raso, Simon, Carpenter

One: Foord, Fowler, Yallop, Luik

After beating the Philippines and Thailand, Gustavsson had only won four of his twenty matches in 90 minutes. He had eighteen months to get it right.

2023.

Boom.

Hosting a World Cup might be a once-in-a-lifetime experience—and we all got to make the most of it. It might even be the reason many of you have any interest in reading this book. Or bought a jersey, discovered a hero, laced a boot or watched a club game.

From July 20 to August 20, Australia and New Zealand were gripped by football.

Tickets were as hard to get as for a Taylor Swift concert.

Where once a Matilda could walk the streets quietly, they were now instantly recognisable.

Like so many moments in this story, our nation got a taste of how the world lives and breathes football. But we hadn't had it quite like this before in our own backyard, and to this level, with sell-out after sell-out, and the most watched television broadcasts in history.

The Matildas' Instagram account blew up, adding 486,000 more fans. People started watching every goal, interview, joke or dance, on repeat.

After the 2022 Asian Cup hiccup, things were simmering nicely again. Heading into a 'farewell friendly' in Melbourne against France, the girls had won eight from nine, and entered the World Cup with a 1-0 win via a Mary Fowler strike in front of 55,000 fans.

If Kerr dominated the billboards, Fowler was heading up the charts with a bullet.

Once proclaimed by Kerr herself as *the next big thing*, Fowler was a talent from an early age. Sport, competition and an active life was at the heart of her upbringing, where she was one of five kids born to her Irish father and Papua New Guinean mum. Life was simple and so too were its pleasures, with most afternoons after school spent at Trinity Beach in Cairns competing with and against her siblings.

Fowler was exposed to elite football early, living in Netherlands from 11 years of age as her talented elder siblings also pursued their football dreams. When she was back in Australia and spotted, she was fast tracked, making her Tillies debut at 15.

Anyone who saw her was taken aback by her talent, technique and humble temperament.

At 16, she signed her first pro deal with Adelaide United (making her debut alongside her sister Ciara); at 17 she was signed by French club Montpellier, and two years later, Manchester City came calling.

She had long been seen as a special talent, but by 2023, her popularity—and importance to her club and country—was skyrocketing.

In fact, since the World Cup, she was even one of just nine global athletes turned into a Barbie doll! How about that, an Aussie kid at 21 years of age having made such an impact to be immortalised alongside world icons like tennis legend Venus Williams or Canadian striker Christine Sinclair.

The hair, the boots and even the gloves were all perfectly replicated. Chosen because she's a role model, it was important to Fowler that the Barbie showcased her at her most comfortable and authentic.

"I wanted to have my Barbie doll replicate when I feel my most confident self and that for me is when I'm on the pitch playing football," Fowler said when it was announced.

She added, "A lot of my biggest moments of growth have come from sport.

"Just the way that I'm able to speak with myself and deal with challenges and the way that I'm able to believe in myself—those are all things that I learned through sport.

"There are so many other things, too, like some of my closest friends I've made through sport."

And the gloves? All of Australia wanted to know about the gloves!

Finally, sheepishly, Fowler explained during the World Cup, "I honestly just like gloves because I get really fidgety.

"So usually I train with a ring on but if it's cold I wear gloves and I can't wear a ring in a match so I usually wear gloves."

Be yourself. Never change, not for anyone.

Twenty-three Australians were blessed with tickets to represent the Matildas on the biggest football stage we've ever seen in this country.

Twenty were at the Asian Cup in India; Chloe Logarzo and Emily Gielnik were the unlucky ones whose races with injury left them just short.

Katrina Gorry's return was a massive in. She is a rare footballer. Watch her closely and you'll admire her intelligence: her passing range, touch, technique and effort. She makes Australia tick.

The Asian Cup in India came not long after having her first child. Her return provided the Matildas with a world-class midfielder, and Australia with a role model the country admired: a mum, and an elite international athlete in a team sport.

When that becomes normal, soon, it will be thanks to stars like Gorry and Tameka Yallop.

Gorry's talent has always sparkled. In 2014, she was named the continent's best player. But after fitness and form issues, daughter Harper Gorry's arrival helped her rediscover her love of the game.

Steph Catley summed up what so many people feel. "I've been so in awe of her." Gorry added to a strong midfield. If there were World Cup questions, it was in defence.

Thankfully, Clare Hunt was a late bloomer who caught the eye with a brilliant season with Western Sydney to become Alanna Kennedy's partner. Hunt was so impressive she was scouted by Paris Saint-Germain afterwards, and has since also moved to England to join Tottenham.

This team, like the Socceroos, is full of so many Aussie stories.

They are you. They are us.

Hunt joined a backline including Ellie Carpenter, getting flashbacks to their days together in Bathurst representative sides. Carpenter, from Cowra, population 10,000, and Hunt from Grenfell with 2,500 people, are two kids from the bush.

There's talent *everywhere* in Australia. Sometimes, you get discovered. Sometimes, like Hunt, you wait a little longer and forge your own journey.

Their message? If we can do it, so can you. If you are fearless.

"It's wonderful that we can both be role models for young kids in country towns, chasing their dream," Hunt told the *Sydney Morning Herald.*

It is hard to believe that Carpenter was still just 23 in 2023. In 2016, at 16, she became the world's youngest female football Olympian and has been on Australia's right side ever since.

Sacrifices her parents made, including moving to Sydney when she was 10, opened doors for their talented daughter. Now, she lives 16,680 kilometres from Cowra, in Lyon, France. There, she showed her determination, battling a year-long rehabilitation to make sure she could live her World Cup dream.

Those two are now regulars alongside veteran Kennedy. It is actually hard to remember a Matildas side that was not marshalled by the towering, skilful defender who made her debut in 2012.

Her call-up came after a season at Newcastle Jets as a 16-year-old. So, like with so many of this new wave of stars, the unsung heroes were Mum and Dad who helped with a drive from Campbelltown to Newcastle, three hours each way, three times a week. It most definitely paid off.

After a distinguished career spanning clubs in Australia, the United States and England, where she is currently with Manchester City, there was a worry that a torrid run with injuries could block the veteran's World Cup dreams.

"I don't think I've ever cried being picked for a team, but I cried on my own later in the day," she said, explaining the relief and emotion of being fit for the tournament.

The team's farewell friendly in Melbourne set the stage: a sell-out, amazing atmosphere and a strong performance. Momentum was swelling as the nation counted down to the opening day of the tournament in Sydney.

What could possibly go wrong …

It was as if every curse that has ever struck Australian football came back to make a really bad joke.

Stadium Australia was buzzing with 75,874 expectant fans PUMPED for the opener against the Republic of Ireland. At the ground, it felt like a momentous night for our country.

All the talk had been about creating an iconic moment for your generation. The Tillies had Cathy Freeman at the 2000 Olympics at the same venue. When she won the 400-metres track and field gold, it was a single moment that stopped all of Australia.

One hour before kick-off, everyone at Stadium Australia stopped again.

This time, they were looking down at their phones as pings and notifications went off.

BREAKING NEWS: SAM KERR OUT WITH INJURED CALF.

This must be a prank.

Somehow, the captain sat in a press conference the day before and kept her painful news secret for the sake of her team.

She must have been gutted, but for her team, she put on a brave face. That's leadership.

For years people asked: what do you do *if*, worst-case scenario, Sam Kerr gets injured?

We were about to find out ...

It would take getting used to, but there was still enough quality with Cortnee Vine coming onto the wing to join Caitlin Foord, Hayley Raso and Mary Fowler in attack.

There's an old saying: *you can't win tournaments in the group stage, but you can lose them.* Australia had a job to do to still be in the tournament when Kerr was ready.

It was nervy. This was the moment, after all, that they'd been focusing on for so long. A packed Olympic Stadium brought chills to so many, especially those players who were playing in front of just a handful of fans not that long ago.

"I had tears in my eyes when we were driving to those games," Catley told the *Sydney Morning Herald.*

It was pure relief when Catley, now the captain, put the hosts up 1-0 seven minutes into the second-half, converting a penalty won by Hayley Raso.

When Kerr's face appeared on the big screen, the crowd erupted. To many, she was the star they knew and came to see.

Without her, they discovered more about a loveable team, now led by one of its most committed players—a stalwart who had been with this group through the under-17s, under-20s, Olympics and now the jewel in the crown.

Arsenal star Catley is a winner, a vibrant spirit that learnt the game playing with her older brother Dan at East Bentleigh Soccer Club before making her W-League debut in her teens. She won five championships (one at Victory, four at City) before moving to the US at 20!

Catley is a leader because she's a role model: selfless, generous, thoughtful and grateful. Before games, she'd think of her family—and how her mum used to fundraise, sell chocolates, or whatever could be done, to ensure she could

Go you good things: the Matildas chase Steph Catley to celebrate a key World Cup goal

play at every level she was talented enough to get to.

"I definitely wouldn't be where I am today without my mum," she said in an interview with the Matildas media in 2024.

Thanks to the new skipper, it was job done. 1-0. The Matildas' first opening game World Cup win since 2007. Move on.

As you'll learn as you embark on your Australian football love affair, it's never straightforward.

First, captain Kerr's calves.

Then, Fowler and Luik got concussed at training and were ruled out for a game.

Next, Nigeria.

A 3-2 loss in Brisbane nearly derailed the entire campaign, making the final group game against Canada a MUST WIN. We couldn't go out in the group stage, could we?

A lead from Emily van Egmond's first-half goal against Nigeria, expertly set up by Foord after a run down the left, lasted just seconds. Nigeria silenced the stadium with the last move before the break.

It was not a good night. At 3-1 down, questions were asked about the coach's tactics, and a World Cup was at risk.

"Frustrated, disappointed," admitted Alanna Kennedy, who scored a late consolation goal.

However, in a way, setting up a knockout game before the knockout stages accidentally electrified the tournament. National interest exploded in support and goodwill to drive the team on. Everyone wanted them to succeed. No one was ready for this adventure to end.

There were enough moments in Brisbane to think all was not lost, but Canada were Olympic gold medallists after all. A tough task.

Naturally, Kerr's fitness became the biggest story in Australia.

Once upon a time, England had fretted over David Beckham's foot in a fit of national frenzy. Sam Kerr's calf became a similar story of national importance in Australia! She did for calf muscles what Beckham did for the fifth metatarsal bone in 2002.

Suddenly, everyone was an expert.

Importantly, Fowler returned and it allowed Foord to move back to the left and reunite with her Arsenal teammate, Catley, down that side. Oh, they were brilliant together.

Responding to pressure, the Matildas could not have been bolder.

The energy in Melbourne quickly turned from fear to fun as Raso banged a first-half brace before Fowler and Catley rounded out a pleasantly surprising thrashing.

It was the night *Ribbons Raso* became a household name. Rightly so. She had just signed to become the first Australian to play for Real Madrid— the biggest football club on the planet.

Her finishing against Canada explained why they wanted her. She was ruthless—and that beaming smile grew wider.

"I fell to my knees, it was so special," said Raso, who knew it was going to be a great night. Raso and her mum, Renaye, both have full moon tattoos. When a full moon lit Melbourne's sky, they both knew it was a sign of things to come.

Ribbons also flew off the shelves across the country with young girls adding the extra kit to their uniforms.

These weren't just fashion items; they had a special meaning for Raso.

The ribbons were a gift from her nan; when she was a shy youngster, it boosted her confidence. As she got older, a ribbon matching her kit's colours became a regular good-luck gift from her nan.

Her World Cup was so good that she was on the Ballon d'Or shortlist with Sam Kerr for the 2023 award for the world's best female footballer, finishing seventeenth in the voting.

It's a performance more remarkable when you learn about her setbacks— at 23 in 2018, she suffered a back injury that she thought could end her career. At Portland Thorns, she broke three vertebrae—bones in your back—which took her six months to recover from. But all that was a distant memory in Melbourne, the night the World Cup exploded.

At parks, cafes, schools, workplaces and dinner tables, you couldn't escape chats about Raso, Foord, Gorry, Fowler, Kerr's calf, and even Gustavsson's tactics.

Football fever had truly gripped the nation.

It was spectacular, extending beyond the Tillies, too. Panama? Jamaica? South Africa? Colombia? It didn't matter. Sell-out. Sell-out. Sell-out.

The world watched Australia's sporting spirit and our unmatched support of elite women's sport.

The display even captured the attention of Premier League royalty. Arsenal legend Ian Wright gushed over Kyra Cooney-Cross's form. "Cooney-Cross bro," he tweeted after her performance against Canada.

Her partnership with Gorry was blossoming in the middle of the park. For the youngster, she hails her experienced sidekick as one of her biggest role models.

"I definitely don't think I'd be where I am ... over the last couple of years without her," she told *News Corp.*

With the amount of TikTok videos that Cooney-Cross appears in alongside Gorry's daughter Harper, she might be able to return the favour—at least in babysitting duties, with both now living in London, playing at Arsenal (Cooney-Cross) and West Ham (Gorry)!

Cooney-Cross catapulted into Matildas contention as a rising star at Melbourne Victory and through Australia's youth sides. Once she started to boss midfields, there was no looking back. In the 2021 grand final she stole the show with a goal directly from the corner flag!

As rumours linked her with a post-World Cup move to Arsenal, their former striker Wright made no secret of the fact that he would love to see her join his former club alongside Catley and Foord.

Her move to the Women's Super League at just 21 years of age meant Cooney-Cross was packing her bags again. Football had already taken her to Hammarby in Sweden, Sydney, Melbourne, Torquay and Ballarat, after growing up in Alice Springs, having moved from Queensland's Sunshine Coast.

With her experience already, it is hard not to see Cooney-Cross smiling in the middle of the park for the next decade or longer and living up to her nickname as the team's serial 'pest' off it.

In Qatar, it was Mat Leckie who broke Danish hearts with a moment of solo brilliance.

In Sydney in the Round of 16, it was Caitlin Foord's turn to knock the European nation out of a World Cup.

In her home state, it was the 29-year-old's moment.

A quiet achiever, world-class talent and Arsenal star, Australia needed Foord to step up in Kerr's absence.

She sure did; she was the game breaker in a game that needed something special to break it open.

It was breathtaking.

Foord started it, deep in her own half. She fed Fowler and sprinted for her life.

Australian players celebrate a dominant 4-0 win vs Denmark in the third group game. From L-R: Katrina Gorry, Clare Hunt, Ellie Carpenter, Mary Fowler, Hayley Raso, Emily Van Egmond

Fowler delivered a dazzlingly inch-perfect pass that left four red shirts behind, before Foord produced a perfect, cool, classy finish through the keeper's legs.

Ruthless. It was the side's only shot of the half. 1-0.

If Denmark did not know what hit them, the deafening noise in the stands told them as Foord ran to them to celebrate.

This was Foord's moment in the spotlight after twelve years as the beating heart of the Matildas' journey. Another star whose mum, Simone, had to fundraise in the early days in Illawarra to support her kid's dreams. The carefree schoolkid mature enough to mark Marta in 2011 was now the superstar on centre stage. The spotlight was hers.

Raso's second-half strike polished a swift team move involving Cooney-Cross, Fowler and van Egmond in the box.

If it was loud for Foord's goal, there was one monstrous cheer to come.

Welcome back, Sam Kerr.

Three hundred and forty-nine minutes late to her own party, Kerr trotted out to test her calf. Sydney went nuts.

So too did Australia, with that game the most watched television program of 2023.

That, we'd find out, was just the warm-up to Matildas mayhem.

The bandwagon headed back to Brisbane for a quarter-final against France.

This stage, a second knockout game, had been the Matildas' historic hurdle, a match they had never conquered.

Australia was not ready for the party to be over!

Mark down the date: August 12, 2023. It's down in the calendar like November 16, 2005.

Iconic.

It is now a night locked in Australian sporting history, a memory so precious there was even talk of building a Tillies statue outside the stadium.

What John Aloisi and Mark Schwarzer were to the Socceroos in 2005, Cortnee Vine and Mackenzie Arnold became to the Matildas.

But first, there was a bonkers game of football. It might have finished 0-0, but it showed how gripping and addictive our game can be—even with no goals.

The VAR disallowed an Alanna Kennedy own goal.

Mackenzie Arnold was astounding.

Steph Catley somehow cleared a goal off the line.

Sam Kerr gave 60 minutes returning from injury.

France legend Wendie Renard had an epic battle with Kerr.

Mary Fowler weaved her magic but was stopped by a goal line block more miraculous than a goalkeeper save.

France subbed their goalkeepers.

Momentum shifted one way, then the other.

Oh, the tension. It was unbearable. And to top it all off, it had to be decided with penalties, the dreaded tie-breaker.

It is a stage where courage is rewarded and legends created.

Time to take a deep breath.

Foord, Kerr and Fowler converted their spot-kicks. Huge. Quality.

When Arnold denied Eve Perisset, the crowd went wild as she grabbed the ball and placed it to take a kick of her own.

If she scored, Australia would be through.

The Matildas team unity was on show as they created history

It felt inevitable that she would. It was her night!

Clank.

Off the woodwork. 3-3. Sudden death. You've got to be kidding!

While we all wilted watching, Gorry, Carpenter and Yallop all somehow kept their cool where a miss would have seen their side eliminated.

HOW DID THEY DO THAT? Their penalties were so precise. They were so damn calm and classy.

Clare Hunt, at 6-6, had the next opportunity to win it, but was denied.

Arnold, Australia's *Minister of Defence,* was thankfully unfazed by her miss and kept making saves.

THREE. SAVES. IN. A. PENALTY. SHOOTOUT.

Actually, she really made four saves, because she had to save one penalty twice. The referee gave France a retake after Arnold was ruled to have left her line early.

6-6. Twenty minutes. A World Cup record for male or female football. No nails left.

Cortnee Vine, your turn. *Vine time.*

The 25-year-old Sydney FC star was one of the quieter squad members, but sport has a truly amazing way of writing stories and providing opportunities.

In a team with players from Real Madrid, Arsenal, Chelsea, Paris Saint-Germain and Lyon, a player from the local A-League Women's competition nailed the most watched goal in Australian football history.

The barrier had been broken. Australia was into the final four of a World Cup. The crowd lost itself in the moment. Social media went berserk revelling in it.

Seventy-five thousand fans in Sydney watched along at Cathy Freeman Park.

There it was. *The moment* the Matildas set out to provide a generation, like Freeman did twenty-four years earlier.

Where were you when Cortnee Vine scored against France?

It changed Vine's life. Front page of the paper. Millions of video views. Sponsors. Photo shoots. A marquee contract with Sydney FC. Helicopter rides.

Cricket with the prime minister. Painted for the Archibald Prize!

It felt like a dream, with a responsibility she relished.

"I have a lot of dads come up to me … and say: 'thank you for what you've done for my daughter'," she said.

Vine's story is special. She wasn't just in the right place at the right time. She put herself there through talent and determination, achieving a goal she put on her door in her childhood home in Brisbane when she was 12.

"Play at a World Cup."

Tick.

Just weeks before the tournament, in front of a then record 9,000 fans, she stayed back way after full-time of the 2023 A-League Women's Grand Final to sign autographs. She even packed spare boots in her bag to give away to fans. Instead of running at the first offer after the World Cup, she remained incredibly true to herself and loyal to the league she had starred in since she was 16.

She wanted to see the 'ripple effect' back home and help drive it, and now, at 26 years of age, is enjoying her first overseas stint with North Carolina Courage of the National Women's Soccer League in America.

Aloisi said he was happy to hand the baton to Vine for Australia's most famous penalty. Schwarzer said Arnold had just produced the nation's greatest goalkeeping performance. Ever.

Decent judges!

France's coach Herve Renard called Arnold a *Goliath* for her display. A giant, at just five feet 11 inches tall.

This was her third World Cup, but her first minutes. She made every second count after timing her run of form perfectly.

"Speechless," she beamed. "Up there with one of the best days of my life."

Her new profile also allowed Arnold's story to be shared widely.

During COVID, she realised her hearing needed attention. With masks on, Arnold could no longer lip read. Her brother Sam had worn hearing aids since he was three and encouraged her to get tested. Rather than hiding, Arnold embraced it, shared her journey, and normalised it. Embrace what life throws at you.

For the Tillies, life had thrown them England.

Mackenzie Arnold

They'd face Australia's greatest sporting rival, the European champions, and many of their Women's Super League clubmates, in the biggest football match in our country's history.

🏐

For some athletes, pressure destroys them.

For the best athletes, the biggest stage is their playground; a chance to share the love they have had for their sport since their childhood by showcasing it to the world. At a World Cup, it is a joy shared with millions of strangers, united by what they experience.

Sixty-three minutes into a World Cup semi-final, Australia—all of Australia— experienced just that.

1-0 down, searching for a way back, the captain took matters into her own hands.

Two of the **Matildas adoring fans** at Stadium Australia

Only Kerr could think of scoring when she received Gorry's pass INSIDE the Matildas' own half.

She surged ahead. Probed. Teased. Surged again, before looking up and unleashing a strike of dreamlike perfection.

The most watched television event in Australia since records were kept witnessed the greatest goal ever scored by an Australian footballer.

Had Kerr scored a tap-in, a World Cup goal on home soil in her first start, it would have been the least she deserved. To be struck by injury on the eve of this tournament was a cruel twist by the football gods. Her teammates rose, and so did she. In public, she was nothing but a leader, even if she was hurting inside.

But Kerr simply does not do ordinary.

Her extraordinary moment was the only thing missing at the World Cup up to that point. Kerr's home World Cup now had a defining moment from its poster girl at the venue of Cathy Freeman's triumph.

It was, strangely, also a consolation.

England were the better side. They rallied after Kerr's goal and regained the lead eight minutes later. At 3-1 by full-time, Australia had met its match, even though Kerr had another golden chance with a header far simpler than the goal she buried.

Despite the loss, we'll always have *that* moment, and despite her tournament not going to plan, Sam Kerr will always have *that* goal.

Spain went on to conquer England in a thrilling decider, while Sweden snared bronze, defeating the Matildas 2-0 in Brisbane in the third-place play-off.

"The way the fans have got behind us, the way girls have carried themselves, I think we've proven to the world we are a footballing nation," Kerr said. "We couldn't get it done tonight, but hopefully we've inspired people for many years to come."

Fourth place was still a record result for an Australian senior side at a World Cup.

The result is now a footnote, because the legacy has been left.

The Next Chapter Is Yours

When my son was born, his 89-year-old great-grandfather bought him a football.

At the time, I thought it was a little bit funny; the ball was almost bigger than he was!

Before I blinked, that ball was being rolled around the house, cuddled, thrown, and finally, kicked. It got weathered, battered and eventually kicked over a fence at a park. The ball was lost but its job was done.

For many, passion for football – not just the ball, or the actual game, or the physical item, but what it means – is passed down from generation to generation. We are blessed in Australia with our lives; but in some parts of the world, football is an escape from reality, the brightest spark of a week. Football can be a hobby, a way to keep fit, or a social activity with friends.

However, for millions around the world, it is a shared experience, a way of life, a community – something that unites, binds and excites you, often with those you love. You go to games together, look forward to it all week, then spend the rest of the week debriefing what happened.

Football is everywhere in Australia, which is wonderful. It is the most-played sport and every park you go to is loaded with people wearing kits that make a rainbow of colours from jerseys from across the planet.

We are starting to see a more prominent sprinkling of gold, especially since the Matildas' recent success. That's incredibly powerful – because these heroes are not from PlayStation games or YouTube. You can follow and be them, because they were once where you are now. Many even play professionally here in our own backyard; so close, you can almost touch them. There are now

Football remains Australia's most participated
grassroots sport: **the potential is limitless**

more Matildas than ever at some of the most famous clubs in the world, while we have decent Socceroos numbers in the Premier League, Bundesliga, Serie A and other top European leagues again for the first time in a while.

When I was growing up, Wembley was the local park where my dad played. It wasn't as easy to follow football like it is today and I grew up knowing very little about Australian football. Once I discovered it, it changed everything. I could watch football from around the planet all day if I could; but it is football here in our own backyard that means that little bit more. I hope this story gives you a taste of that passion and a little window into the world of Australian football.

This book is just one layer of a deep Australian football story, which is never short of a twist or turn. At the time of publishing, the Matildas are on the hunt for a new coach after a disappointing Olympics in Paris, while Graham Arnold resigned as Socceroos boss after a poor start to the qualifying path to the 2026 World Cup in the USA, Canada and Mexico, replaced by Tony Popovic.

The best thing about sport? There is always hope. Never stop dreaming. Just listen to Popovic, who wants to build a green and gold side that "play better than the Socceroos have ever played". I'm here for that.

"I was always brought up that anything is possible from my parents; I've had that as a young player, I had that as a senior player, I had that as a coach," Popovic said when announced as coach.

"I always dreamed it is possible, this role.

"Now I am dreaming it is possible that we come first in the (qualifying) group; I am dreaming that it is possible to do something special at the World Cup. But I also know dreams are just one part...you have to work. We have to work at a standard, at an elite level, that gives us the opportunity to do something special."

The story of our World Cups and the modern journey of our Socceroos and Matildas is a great introduction to who we are as a football nation and what we could become, but it doesn't even scratch the surface.

There is a lot of work to do and a long way for the game and our country to go to reach its potential.

"We just haven't understood the football significance of things," Ange Postecoglou once told *Optus Sport*. "The soul of football. What it can do. What it can mean."

That's now for you to explore and discover both on and off the park.

Or maybe you're writing the next chapters right now, but with your feet, inspired by the path set by the legends of our game.

"We shouldn't just dream of qualifying for the World Cup," Johnny Warren famously said.

"We should aspire to win it."

Johnny Warren MBE OAM (1943-2004),
1974 Socceroo, who showed us how to believe

Acknowledgements

Thank you Cooper for the idea, Teya for the encouragement and my wife Tali for embracing this passion project and not just indulging your boys' interest in football, but being a part of it. For the addiction, I go back to my late grandfather, who imported the bug from Budapest, giving it to my father, uncle, brother and I. Grateful.

Reading, writing and football are three of my favourite things; to combine them all to share my passion and try spread the gospel (of football, but also encouraging children to read) has been a rewarding and refreshing exercise.

Thank you to Bonita Mersiades from Fair Play Publishing, a great champion for football and believer in football storytelling, for your immediate enthusiasm in this idea, continued support through the process and production of a beautiful book put together by Leslie Priestley. Football storytelling is an untapped treasure trove in Australia in all formats but Fair Play is doing a remarkable job in the book publishing space.

Big thanks go to the wonderfully talented photographer and champion of football Aleksandar Jason (@thatfootballphotog) for generously supporting this work with spectacular imagery from the Women's World Cup in 2023, which freeze those special moments in time for prosperity. Some of the most iconic moments in recent Australian football history have been captured by Aleks' lens in a way only someone with his unique knowledge and passion can deliver.

I've had some great help along the way with this book. Thanks to Tim Briscoe for a football fanatic and school teacher's point of view and brilliant edit of the first version of this script and Jake Rosengarten for your forensic look at the final version.

To Simon Hill and Andy Harper, the voices calling so many of these iconic moments, thank you for providing a final sense check. I have been blessed to have met wonderful, interesting, passionate people through my career and a couple of trips with those two during the Fox Sports days, where I learnt plenty about the Socceroos, are some of my favourite memories.

So too were the early mornings spent watching football and doing punditry with John Aloisi, Heather Garriock and others at Optus Sport, where I learnt much about the game, the complexities of our history, and heard plenty of great stories. Is there a story without the contributions of those two? I am so grateful and humbled by your support for this concept.

This is by no means a definitive history of the national teams or the sport in Australia, but simply, a cracking story about brilliant Australian men and women with plenty of plot twists and turns, as well as lessons, for young readers and blossoming football fans. For parents, I hope it brings back memories, sparks a nice conversation with your kids, or you even find out a new fun fact along the way.

The only atmosphere and moment of roof-raising noise I have experienced like that night in November 2005, where I watched as a wide eyed teen with my dad and brother, was when Cortnee Vine scored against France in Brisbane. Indeed, reporting and reflecting on that game and the journey from Aloisi's breakthrough in 2005 to the explosion of football mania in 2023 was one of the catalysts for this book.

In between there have been highs, plenty of lows but put it all together and it is one heck of a story. Our story. I hope you enjoyed reading it.

About the Author

David Weiner is an award-winning content leader who has devoted much of his 17-year career to football.

As editor of Fox Sports Football and Optus Sport, and then Director of Content at the A-Leagues, he has built and led digital brands that passionately told Australian football stories across written editorial, audio, social, video, broadcast and original content formats. Having been captivated by the global game in his teens, he was able to share that joy with audiences through his work, particularly when part of broadcasts for the UEFA Champions League, Women's World Cup, Euros and Copa America tournaments.

However, David's belief in the importance of Australian football - and telling its stories - remains one of his driving passions.

This book was encouraged and inspired by his son, who is a seven-year-old football fanatic. It also helped him rediscover his own joy and belief in the sport at a time when the complexities of the local game deeply challenged it.

David lives in Sydney with his wife and two children. His eldest is frighteningly on track to know more about the sport than he does!

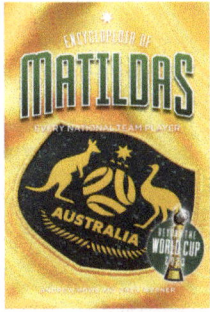

Encyclopedia of Matildas
Beyond the World Cup 2023

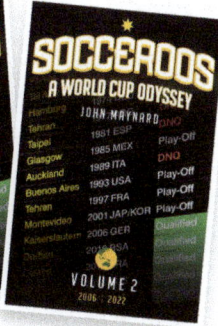

Socceroos – A World Cup Odyssey,
1965 to 2022 Volumes 1 and 2

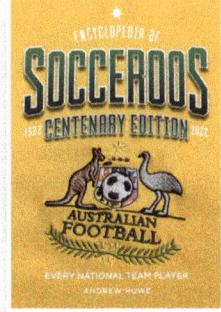

Encyclopedia of Socceroos
Centenary Edition

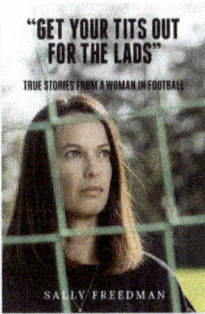

"Get Your Tits Out
for the Lads"

George Best
Doen Under

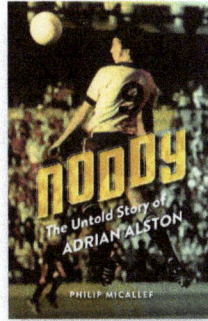

Noddy, The Untold Story
of Adrian Alston

Football Fans
In Their Own Write...

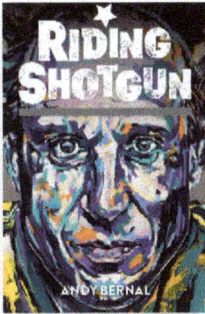

Riding Shotgun

The First Matildas

The Agents' Game

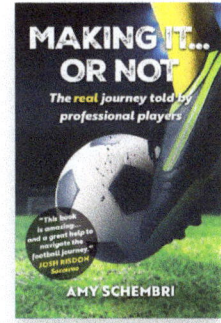

Making It... Or Not

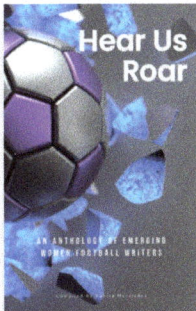

Hear Us Roar – An
anthology of emerging
women football writers

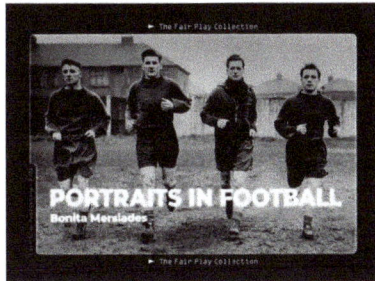

Portraits In Football

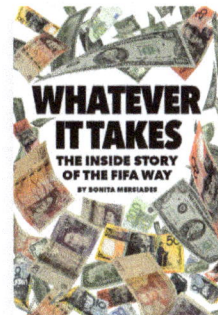

Whatever It Takes
The Inside Story of
The FIFA Way

fairplaypublishing.com.au

9 781923 236158